Bombs and Lambs

Bombs and Lambs

Margaret Monkman

VANTAGE PRESS
New York

FIRST EDITION

Published by Vantage Press, Inc.
419 Park Avenue South, New York, NY 10016

Manufactured in the United States of America
ISBN: 978-0-533-16157-7

Library of Congress Catalog Card No.: 2008910073

0 9 8 7 6 5 4 3 2 1

To my husband, Dick,
and to Richard and Mary, who both had lambs

Disruption

Early in August of 1939 our family, my mother and father, two elder brothers, Harold and Gordon, my younger brother, Richard, and I, went for our usual three week holiday at the seaside. Bude is a small town in northwest Cornwall, which we loved for its beautiful beaches where we could play for hours when the tide was out: building sand castles, watching for creatures in the little pools left when the tide ebbed, or clambering over rocks to see what we might find. Where we would all have family games of cricket with three to a team; and where, when the tide was coming in, those who could swim, our parents and Harold and Gordon, could take surfboards (not the big kind used now but small ones, different sizes for people of different sizes) and catch waves as they broke, riding them, flat on the board, all the way to the shallow water. Richard and I couldn't wait for when we could swim and be able to surf too.

It wouldn't be that year. We had been there for less than a week when it became almost inevitable that there would be a war, and our parents realized that we must return to London. Everything was hurriedly packed into the car; our father, whom we'd never heard swear, wrote succinctly in the guest book, "Damn Hitler," and we left.

For most of the rest of what should have been school holidays, we went to school each morning and returned home each afternoon. I don't remember my class having

1

many lessons but do remember being supplied with a gas mask each, and being told that we must be sure to have it with us at all times. Harold and Gordon had to do that too. Richard was the one of us who took the rules for gas masks most seriously. One evening, when he had gone upstairs to get undressed for his bath, the telephone rang. It was somebody asking to speak to Richard, so our mother called up the stairs, "Richard, you have a phone call." It was probably his first one ever. In a moment down he came, with no clothes on and his gas mask hanging on his shoulder. Looking even smaller than he did completely dressed, he went into the study to answer the phone. The caller had a wrong number.

When we came home from school, since nobody had homework, we'd often have a makeshift game of cricket in the back garden, trying not to hit the ball into the neighbours' garden on one side or the church on the other and, especially, trying not to hit it over the netting our father had put between the lawn and the house in an effort to prevent Harold and Gordon from breaking windows. Richard and I couldn't hit that hard.

We did this all through the rest of August while the news made it more and more inevitable that we could not avoid war. Even so, I think we all went to bed on August 31st expecting the next day to be very much like those of the past three weeks.

In a sudden urge to lift a boulder I felt I had been carrying for fifty years, I wrote this on September 1st, 1989, the fiftieth anniversary of the mass evacuation of children from London, two days before World War II began.

Fifty Years Ago

We have all seen and read many stories of war, but I want to recount another, simply and straightforwardly, because it is so clear in my memory even after fifty years. And because I looked at my children when they were the age I was then and at my grandchildren as they approached that age, wishing fervently that no children should have such an experience ever again. Unfortunately, many do—and far worse. Mine is by no means a horror story, but it is a story that encapsulates some of the lesser misery that war can cause.

Fifty years ago on September 1st, thousands of children, with luggage labels attached to their blouses or blazers, were packed into hundreds of trains and shipped out of London. Neither they nor their parents or teachers knew where they were headed, just that it was out of London. There was not yet war, but it was plain that it could no longer be avoided, and Hitler was expected to launch an air attack the minute war was declared.

So for weeks of what should have been our summer holidays, we had been going to school each morning with gas masks slung over our shoulders and rucksacks full of a change of clothes on our backs. Sometimes we would file through a gas-filled truck to have our masks tested. Every day we would have an air-raid drill and at a signal crouch beneath our desks. Always we'd wonder whether we would go home at the end of the day.

On September 1st we didn't. That morning Harold and Gordon left before us, as they always did, since their school was further away. When Richard and I left, our mother watched, waving for as long as we kept turning to wave back, all the way to where we had to turn the corner. We'd done this every morning and every afternoon for those past weeks. On other days we had returned in the late afternoon. Not that day. As soon as we reached the school playground, we were lined up by classes. Then, fortunately, younger children were allowed to join their older siblings. My five-year-old brother came to stand by me. I was seven and rapidly growing much older.

In a long crocodile, two by two, we set off to walk the mile or more to the railway station. Soon Richard's pack was too heavy for him, and I had to ease the load by hoisting from beneath with one hand while lifting on the straps of my own with the other hand. We trudged along the familiar streets, bewildered and scared, and soon everyone was hot and thirsty and close to tears.

But once we reached the station platform, our mood changed to one of excitement and a spirit of adventure, as though we were off to the zoo with lots of children all looking like us, who also carried gas masks, rucksacks and luggage labels. Trains whizzed by packed with more children, staring at us as we stared back. Train after train passed, until at last an empty one drew up. We jostled for places as kindly teachers stowed our rucksacks beneath seats or stuffed them on racks.

Somehow, though, those packs, unwieldy and heavy as they had been, had represented security. Without them we didn't feel safe. Besides, the train was drawing out of the familiar station, and none of us knew where it was going. To add to our uneasiness, it soon seemed that the engine driver didn't know either, for we would pull into a station, shunt out, pull back in and reverse again. It was hours before a place was finally found for us to alight, tired and once more on the verge of tears.

Yet up to now had been the easy part. Now the surroundings became strange to urban children. In retrospect, I think we must have been set down at a terminal where small farmers sent their produce to be shipped to urban markets. The track ended in the middle of fields by a big shed that smelled of lettuces and early apples. Today, however, it was lined with trestle tables topped by neat rows of brown paper bags. Filing past, we were each issued one and told that they contained our iron rations: hardtack, condensed milk and a small, black tin of mysterious tablets, on which we were said to be able to survive for days, should no food be available; hardly reassuring news to frightened children. Next we were given a thick, grey, scratchy blanket and struggled to carry everything with us onto a waiting bus.

Our family had often gone for walks in the country, but to many of the children the winding lanes between high, late summer hedgerows, and the small village of centuries old houses, which turned out to be our destination, was a totally foreign environment. There we were to be abandoned by our last link with our old world. We were ushered into the village hall to be sat in a large circle. Our teachers had suddenly vanished, we didn't know where. Soon two women came around serving cups of tea. For me this posed a question. Luckily we were a long way round from where they started. What should I do? Richard didn't like tea, but I knew he wouldn't say so, just sit there and not drink it. I didn't think they would like that, but there was time for me to gather my courage and tell them, hoping they would offer him something else, but there was nothing else.

Meanwhile many other women were walking around the circle looking us over and deciding who they would choose to be their foster child or children. It was much, I discovered later in the war, like farmers selecting cattle at the market. We saw other children being selected, but the women kept passing us by until we were the only ones left. What was going to happen to us? Then suddenly someone came hurrying out of the kitchen, where she had been in charge of making the tea, and straight up to us. "Hello," she said, "I hope you'll come home with me." By now, in spite of her friendly overtures, we were petrified and rode the last stage of our journey, up a hill and some way out of the village, unable to respond in any way.

Most of the rest of the day is a blur, other than that for lunch we had some of our strange, "iron rations," then immediately sat at the kitchen table to write letters home telling where we were. Richard's letter was pictures captioned by me, with a long row of hugs and kisses at the end. Mine, I think, contained only the necessary information, but also had a row of hugs and kisses. We wondered whether Harold and Gordon had been evacuated too and, if so, where they were and if they were writing letters.

It was a long afternoon, for our hostess too, I'm sure. No children lived there. There were no toys. The outside world was an alien one to us that later we would come to revel in, but not that day, and although the young couple who had so suddenly become our foster parents were very kind, they were certainly unprepared for an instant family. So it was probably a relief to us all that English children went to bed before the birds.

Except that bedtime far from home is the hardest time for young children. The room was strange, sparsely furnished, with a curtainless window which looked out on deep woods. Our arrival had been so unexpected that there were no sheets. We climbed into the one single bed, under the rough army blanket we had been issued earlier, and hugged each other, while Richard cried himself to sleep, and I tried desperately to swallow the lump in my throat.

Journal

Yesterday, when I unpacked our rucksacks, I found a notebook and a note from Mummy. That almost made me cry, but her note helped me swallow the tears. She said how much she and Daddy were going to miss us all and, as soon as possible, when they had learned where we were, they would come to see us. Then she explained about the notebook. She thought it might help me not feel so bad if I wrote about what was happening to Richard and me. Just writing that has helped.

This morning when we woke up, as Uncle Bill revved his motor bike and drove off, we weren't sure where we were, but then it all came rushing in, and Richard started to cry. I wanted to but knew he needed me not to. It helps a lot that the people we are billeted on are very kind. They haven't any children, but they seem pleased to have us. They are Mr. and Mrs. Turner, but they have asked us to call them Auntie Grace and Uncle Bill, so we don't feel abandoned the way we did yesterday, when nobody seemed to want us. We were the last children sitting in the empty village hall, until Mrs. Turner (Auntie Grace) came hurrying from the kitchen, where she was in charge of the tea we'd all, except Richard, been given.

At breakfast Auntie Grace said, "Well, your mother

and father should have your letters by now, so they know where you are, and I expect they will write to you today." She continued, "I looked in on you before we went to bed and realized that one of the first things we have to do is find some sheets and look for another bed. I think Uncle Bill's mother and father probably have an extra one. Richard's lip trembled. He didn't want a separate bed, not yet anyhow. "I'm sure they will lend us some sheets until I can go into Maidstone and buy some. I asked Uncle Bill to stop on his way home to ask them."

It's a beautiful day, so after breakfast we went outside to explore a bit, but when we reached the woods that looked so deep and dark last night they still did, and we weren't so sure we wanted to go into them. Then, just as we turned to go back into the house, a big boy walked through the front gate and came over to us. His name is Lionel, and he lives on a farm just across the road. He'd seen us arrive yesterday with Auntie Grace, but his mother told him to wait until this morning to come over to say, "Hello." He's much older than us and knows lots about birds. He said, "I'll take you for a walk if you like, and I bet we'll see some you've never seen before." Auntie Grace said, "All right, but take good care of them, Lionel, and don't go too far." So we set off through the woods, which didn't seem nearly as scary with him there, and then there were fields.

Lionel kept stopping, whispering, "Shush, shsh," then pointing to a bird we hadn't noticed. "That's a chaffinch," he'd say if he thought we didn't know. We didn't know many, really, only the ones we'd see in our back garden: robins and blackbirds and starlings and sometimes a thrush. In only about half an hour, he showed us the chaffinch, a bullfinch, some noisy jays, and one bright yellowhammer. Then, when we were coming back a dif-

8

ferent way, along a stream, he showed us funny little black and white water-wagtails that kept bobbing up and down, the way Richard and I do sometimes when we have baths together, putting our heads right down into the water. Going for the walk with Lionel was fun and almost made us forget about missing Mummy and Daddy and Harold and Gordon so much.

After lunch Richard was very tired from our walk and had a nap, so while I was waiting for him to wake up, I did some puzzles that Uncle Bill had found on the children's page of his newspaper and began writing this, my first journal entry. Mummy was right, doing this does help me not to think quite so much about wanting to be at home. Then just after Richard woke up, and while we were wondering what to do for the rest of the afternoon, we heard a car drive in, and Auntie Grace said, "Who can that be?" We could hardly believe our eyes. It was our car! We ran straight out and were jumping up and down, as excited as could be, as Mummy and Daddy got out. We hugged and kissed, swapping around from one to the other and never wanting to let go, but then we realized that Auntie Grace had come out and was waiting to meet them and ask them to come in. We couldn't let go of their hands, but somehow we all managed to squeeze through the door into the kitchen.

The rest of the afternoon's a blur. I know they'd been to see Harold and Gordon on their way here. They are in Tunbridge Wells, so we are all in Kent. Our letters had arrived with the morning post and, immediately, they'd looked at a map and set out. It's lucky it was Saturday, so Daddy didn't have to go up to London. It was awful when they had to leave, though, but they said they would do their best to come next week end. A whole week sounds like a very long time not to see them!

Journal

I'm so glad that Mummy gave me this notebook and suggested that when I was feeling homesick I could write in it, and it might help me feel a bit better. I really do need to write in it now. Yesterday I sent Richard home alone on the bus. I'd asked Auntie Grace if she thought that would be all right. I'm getting a bit tired of looking after him all the time. I saw him onto the bus, and he knows where to get off now. Auntie Grace said she would go to meet him. That meant I could go to play with Joan, a friend from my class. We had a good time playing with Joan's dolls until Mrs. Baker, Joan's foster mother, called up the stairs, "Joan, it's nearly time for supper," and I knew I'd be dreadfully late for mine unless I really hurried home, well, not *home,* but up the hill to Auntie Grace and Uncle Bill's.

When we were out with Lionel the other day, we went down to the village on a footpath that went through fields. I thought it was shorter than the road (it isn't) and decided to go back that way. Oh, I do wish I hadn't. As I was walking along the edge of a field where the wheat had been cut and was lying in rows, waiting to be made into sheaves, I saw lots of flies on something and went over to see what it was. There was a big, dead lamb with none of

10

its wool, except on its head, and the flies, huge ones, were swarming all over it in a great, buzzing crowd. I was nearly sick and started to run along the path to get away from it. Only I kept hearing the flies all the way back to Auntie Grace and Uncle Bill's. I wished so much that I was going home instead.

Auntie Grace wasn't pleased that I was late. "Where have you been? You had me worried." I murmured, "Sorry," and sat down to the supper she'd kept hot for me. I tried, but I couldn't eat it. Instead of meat and peas and potatoes, I saw fat flies. Auntie Grace asked, "What's the matter? Are you all right?" I couldn't tell her and was almost crying. I just wanted to go home and tell Mummy. She's right. It does help to write about it.

Saturday
A day or two later

Mummy and Daddy can't come this weekend, so here I am again. Today it's drizzling, and we haven't been out much. Richard's playing on the floor with his soldiers. It's quiet, and I can write for a while.

Yesterday we were both late for supper and Auntie Grace said, "You'll have to ask someone to tell you when it's time to go home. I worry when you're late. Now it's been twice that this has happened." In the morning we had asked her if we could go and play with Mary and Jimmy after school. They're just about the same ages as we are. Mary's in my class and Jimmy's in Richard's. They're billeted on a farm and wanted to show us the animals. It was almost as good as going to the zoo, and these animals are all useful. Even the cats are only there because they catch rats and mice, and the dog is a sheepdog.

11

Mary said, "He's very clever at making all the sheep come into a big blob, so that you can't tell where one ends and the next one begins."

It was afternoon milking time, and we watched two men who work on the farm milking the cows. It looked easy. "So it be, once you 'ave the knack," one of them told us and went on filling up the bucket he'd put under the cow. The milk made a lovely pinging sound as it hit the sides.

After that the boys went off to play by themselves, and Mary went in to fetch her skipping rope. We started taking it in turns, but then we decided to try both skipping in the same rope, taking it in turns to have the rope or be the one to run in. As we did it, we tried to say all of one of the rhymes we say if we're playing with other girls in the playground.

My mother says I never should
Play with the gypsies in the wood.
If I did, she would say,
"Naughty little girl to disobey."

It wasn't nearly as easy running in and out as it was only a shortish rope, but we hadn't been trying very long when Mrs. Johnson came to the farmhouse door and called, "Mary, Jimmy, it's time to come in and wash your hands for supper." Oh, no, Richard and I would be really late. It was about half a mile to our billet.

We ran out onto the road but couldn't keep running for long. I began walking fast, but Richard lagged further and further behind, so I had to keep turning around to see if he was still coming. Then we came to a stretch where one side of the road was all dark woods. We hadn't been there before, but the village children had told us about it.

They said, "The gypsies live there. Yer don't wanna be walking on that road when it's dark. They'll come outa the woods and catch yer." It wasn't dark yet, but the woods made it almost dark. I knew Richard wouldn't come at all if I didn't wait for him, so I had to, though I was frightened, too, and kept hearing in my head, "I never should play with the gypsies in the wood." Somehow we got by there, running and walking and running again, until we both had stitches in our sides. At last we turned the corner and could see Auntie Grace and Uncle Bill's house just down the road. In spite of our stitches, we ran up to the front gate and quickly into the house. Of course Auntie Grace wasn't very pleased with me for being late again, but as soon as she saw our faces, she said, "Well, never mind this time. What's the matter? Are you all right? You both look as if you saw a ghost."

When we told her why we'd been scared, she said, "Those village children. Don't listen to them. They're trying to frighten you. They know there aren't any gypsies in those woods. Even if there were, they wouldn't hurt you. They'd be made to move on if they ever did anything like that. Now, don't worry. Come and have supper before it's ruined." Then, when Uncle Bill came home, he let us sit one on each knee and told us that when he was little, he was scared, but then some gypsies came sometimes to help on his family's farm; they talked a different language, which might be why village children thought they were scary. He said what Auntie Grace had said, "There haven't been gypsies in those woods for years."

By the time we had to go to bed we felt much better.

Journal

October 19th was Richard's birthday. When we woke up, he was on the edge of tears; it was a weekday, so Mummy and Daddy wouldn't be able to come. He thought they'd forgotten. I hugged him and said, "You know they couldn't possibly do that. Happy Birthday! Come on let's dress and go down to breakfast." As soon as we were at the bottom of the stairs, Auntie Grace called out, "Happy Birthday, Richard, and Many Happy Returns of the Day. Come and see what's here for you." Sure enough, on the table at Richard's place, were three envelopes, which he opened straight away, not thinking of food at all.

There was a card from Mummy and Daddy with lots of Os and Xs and a message that they'd be here on Saturday with a birthday cake. Auntie Cissy and Auntie Jessie had each sent cards and some money to spend on what he would like. They weren't sure what that would be. The last card was from Harold and Gordon and told him that Mummy said she would pack their present with hers and Daddy's. Auntie Grace said, "There now, you certainly weren't forgotten! Come on, eat your breakfast or you'll miss the bus." At home we always had one present at breakfast, so I had given mine, a Mars bar, to Auntie Grace yesterday, and that was waiting at his place with the cards. He liked it, but I could tell he was disappointed that there wasn't a present from Mummy and Daddy. Still, he managed to eat something and, by running most of the way we just caught the bus. On the way home the day before, I had managed to tell the other children on the bus that today would be his birthday, and as we got on there was a chorus of "Happy Birthday"s.

When we arrived back in the afternoon, Auntie Grace said, "Richard, look what's come for you!" On the table there was a big cardboard box addressed to him. "It arrived soon after you left. Come on. Let's see what's in it." She handed him scissors, (showing him she realized he was a year older and could manage by himself). It was full of things Mummy and Daddy had known he would like, as well as a warm red pullover Grandma had knitted for him and crayons from Harold and Gordon. The thing he liked most was a beginners set of meccano.* Harold and Gordon have quite a lot at home, but he was delighted to have his own. Right at the bottom of the box there was a new hairbrush for me, just like Mummy's, and a note that said, "To help you get the tangles out. Lots of love, Mummy and Daddy." Mummy always gives a present to those of us who aren't having a birthday. Now it was all unpacked, and Auntie Grace said, "There's still time for us to go for a walk before I have to cook dinner. Come on; let's go while the sun's still shining." We set off straight up the road, past the bus stop and on further, where we hadn't been yet. Soon we came to some big woods. We wouldn't have dared to go in alone, but with Auntie Grace we felt safe. We hadn't gone far when she stooped to pick up some-

*meccano in England is like an erector set in the U.S.

thing. It was not quite round and was smooth and hard. Then we saw there were lots more, but some were almost covered with prickles that hurt. She told us they were chestnuts. "Fill your pockets and we'll roast some after dinner. Come on, there won't be any dinner if we don't hurry back." Soon after we were there, we heard Uncle Bill's motor bike. He came in the door saying, "Happy Birthday, Richard."

At dinner, there was a birthday cake, with six candles to blow out, that Auntie Grace had made in the morning. As soon as we had finished, she said, "Now we'd better roast our chestnuts." We all sat round the fire, while Auntie Grace put some chestnuts in the coals. That made little sparks fly up the chimney, and she told us that she and her sisters had loved to watch them and called them little soldiers. After a few minutes Uncle Bill reached for the tongs to turn the chestnuts over. Soon they decided it was time to try one or two, peeled a few and gave us one each, warning that if they felt hot to our fingers, we'd better wait a bit or we'd burn our tongues. When they had cooled a little, we sprinkled some salt on them and tasted. They were delicious and not like anything we'd ever tasted before.

We couldn't possibly eat them all in one evening. Auntie Grace promised, "We'll have more tomorrow. Now it's time you were in bed. Off you go. Sleep well." On the way upstairs, Richard said, "I missed Mummy and Daddy and the boys, but that was fun." I hope we can make little soldiers again tomorrow.

Journal

We have lots and lots more snow than Richard and I have ever seen, so we can't go to school. It's a week now since we went. That should be fun, but Mummy and Daddy can't come for the weekends while the roads are so bad. They are covered with snow and even the ones that have been cleared a bit are very narrow.

The day before yesterday, since we'd all been in the house for days on end, Auntie Grace said, "Let's go for a walk along the part of the road that's been cleared," so we all bundled up, searched for some mittens that we hadn't seen all that week, and out we went. It was strange; we walked between two very high banks of snow, so high it felt as though we were in a tunnel, but a tunnel with a far off blue roof!

Yesterday was another beautiful day. We went out right after breakfast to see if we could make a snowman. Before long Margaret and Raymond, the evacuees from next door, came out, too, shouting, "Wow! We're out, we're out! Isn't, this wonderful! What are you going to do?"

"Well, we thought we'd make a snowman, only we don't know how to. Do you?"

"No. There's never enough snow. How could we?"

None of us had any idea how to begin, but we had seen pictures, so we knew we had to start with lots of snow for the body. The most snow was just by the front gate where it had been piled up from the road, so that's where we went. It wouldn't stay together, though, so I ran in to ask Auntie Grace if she knew how to do it. "Well, what we used to do was make a snowball, then keep rolling it in more and more snow until it was really big. Try that."

We did, and it worked, so we went on to make his head. Then, of course, we needed to find some stones for his eyes. We were all grubbing around in the snow, trying to dig far enough down when a loud voice behind us said, "Good morning, Father Breadon." Startled out of our wits, we spun round, and there, right behind us, sitting high up on his horse was the Rector, waiting for us to say, "Good morning, Father Breadon"! We all chorused, "Good morning, Father Breadon," because he looked as if he'd stay there until we did. He rode right off, luckily, because we were all bursting with laughter. It seemed so silly.

We went back to digging for stones and soon Raymond fished out two, but how could we make a nose? While we were thinking it would be impossible, Auntie Grace, who'd watched from the window, came out with a carrot and even an old hat and scarf of Uncle Bill's. Now we had a lovely snowman, just like the ones we'd seen in pictures! He looked so real we thought the Rector should come back to say, "Good morning, Father Breadon," to him.

That was fun, but still Mummy and Daddy haven't been able to come. It's been four weeks now since the last time we saw them and seems ages and ages. Bedtime is the hardest, so I have to try to comfort Richard when I'm longing for home too. Our snowman is beginning to look rather shabby, and we'd hoped and hoped they'd be able to see him. We're wondering whether Harold and Gordon made one too.

It's cold, but we can't have a good warm fire because the coal man can't deliver until the roads are cleared. There isn't much hot water either, so before we go to bed we share a basin of water to wash in. Auntie Grace comes up to help us, though she didn't do that when we could have baths. One night, as she helped, she said, "I think I'm going to have to have a baby when you're not here to be my children." Somehow, I don't know why, that was comforting to hear when we were missing Mummy and Daddy so much.

Two Weeks Later

Hurrah! At last the roads are cleared. Mummy and Daddy will be able to come at the weekend. We're even glad the bus we take to school can run again.

Journal

There's a boy in my class who looks as good as good can be, but he's always being naughty and has to stand in the corner. He used to sit at the back of the class behind a girl with plaits, but he dipped one of them in his inkwell, so now he sits at the front. Only the minute Miss Anderson turns to write on the board, he throws little pellets he's made by chewing bits of paper. Sometimes, if he keeps being naughty, Miss Anderson sends him to the headmistress, and she canes him, but even that doesn't stop him for long.[*] Well, I said he looks angelic, and Mrs. Breadon must have thought he really was. When we first arrived and were in the village hall, she chose him as the evacuee for her and Father Breadon to have at the Rectory. I think George's parents must be feeling sorry for him being there. Last Friday they brought him a bicycle!

The next afternoon he came up the hill to ride where it's flat and to show off. None of us had ever ridden a bicycle and kept asking for a turn. Margaret and Raymond from next door tried first, but Mrs. Hawley came right out to call them into the house.

Then Richard had a turn, but his legs were too short,

---

[*]This isn't allowed now but was quite common then. Thank goodness it never happened to us.

so at last I could try. It was wonderful! To start me going, George ran alongside holding the saddle, but not for long, and there I was riding all by myself; only I was beginning to feel bad about Richard. He'd been sitting at the edge of the road just watching while George held the saddle to help me, and I realized that, even if Richard couldn't reach the pedals, he could have a ride now and then. So George and I ran one on each side, holding the bike steady while we pushed. He loved that, and after a while went happily in to tell Auntie Grace about it. George and I rode up and down that flat stretch of road ever so many times. Then George rode without holding the handlebars. So I tried. At first I had to keep grabbing them quickly, but soon I could do it! I stretched my arms out from my sides and felt as if I was flying. Soon though, George left, and I went in for tea. Shaking her head, Auntie Grace said, "I couldn't believe my eyes. No hands on your first day!"

The trouble is George hasn't been back with the bike. The Rector has found a way to make him behave. When George isn't being good, he takes the bike away for a day. Poor George. He does love that bicycle, but I doubt if he can manage to be good *all* the time.

Saturday was my birthday, which was lucky because Mummy and Daddy could come in the afternoon after they'd seen Harold and Gordon. They brought a birthday cake, with icing and eight candles, and lots of presents, including a lovely new summer frock, which I put on straight away. Of course, what I wanted most was a bicycle, but they didn't know about my learning to ride until they came. Anyhow it wouldn't have been possible. There are four of us and only one of George. Harold and Gordon gave me a box of crayons, which was especially good because Mummy always gives a present to those of us who aren't having a birthday, and that's what she gave Richard, so now he won't have to keep using mine. From Auntie Grace and Uncle Bill, there was a pretty purse on a shoulder strap. I'll be able to take our milk money to school in it. Mummy had made more clothes for my doll Petite, a summer dress just like mine, a cardigan and some socks. She looks very smart now. Most of my other presents were books, which really thrills me because the library van from Maidstone only comes every two or three weeks. My favourite is the one from Auntie Jessy. It is poems chosen by a mother for her daughter, who has been evacuated to Canada. There are two poems I love; they are both by William Blake, one is called *The Lamb* and the other *The Tyger*. They're very different from each other. I read *The Lamb* to Richard but wasn't sure he'd like *The Tyger*. It might give him nightmares. He does have them sometimes and has to come into bed with me, which keeps me awake because he kicks in his sleep.

Richard sat on Mummy's lap almost all the time she was here, which he mostly does when they come. I like to snuggle up to Daddy. We're very lucky they can come so often (except when there's a snowstorm!). We were both sad yesterday afternoon when they left. As we walked out to the car, I suddenly felt older than eight and said to Mummy, "Being eight's like being forty, isn't it?" She looked right into my eyes and gave me a big hug, saying, "Yes. Yes, I suppose it is."

After we'd waved until they turned the corner, we went in to use our separate boxes of crayons. Auntie Grace used some too. She's good at drawing and made a lovely picture of a house that looked like this one and had smoke coming out of the chimney. Even though she's very kind to us, we still wish we could go home.

Journal

Mummy is here because Auntie Grace is having an operation. We're sorry she's ill but glad, glad, GLAD that Mummy is with us for more than just a weekend. We're doing all sorts of things we didn't do before the war. For one thing, we listen to the news on the wireless with her, right after The Children's Hour.

It isn't good, except that now Mr. Churchill is Prime Minister. He made a wonderful speech in Parliament, saying that things are going to be hard, that we'll have "blood, sweat, toil, and tears," but that we, everybody, will fight back with all our might and surely won't give in. Somehow he has made everyone feel better because he seems so strong. Our army has had to retreat from Europe. Anybody who had a boat which could possibly be used went across the channel to Dunkirk to rescue as many of the soldiers as possible. Hitler is saying that the Germans will invade England soon. The church bells all over the country aren't going to ring any more unless it's to warn people that there is an invasion. We asked Mummy, "What'll happen if we are in school?" She said, "I'll come running down the hill to fetch you, and I'll bring the carving knife in case there are any Germans already here." Having her here helps us not to be afraid.

Perhaps we can hide in the woods. Auntie Grace took us there once not long ago. She called them woods, but I thought it was more like a forest. They'd make a good place to hide. We went there to pick primroses, and there were so many they looked like a big yellow carpet. We picked lots, but you couldn't tell any were gone. When we came home Auntie Grace helped us pack some in shoe boxes, with lots of damp newspaper around them. We sent some to our neighbour at home, Mrs. Greensmith, because she loves them so much, and another box to Grandma.

*   *   *

At last it's stopped raining, and the sun's coming out. There's almost enough blue sky to make a sailor a pair of trousers. We're going to go for a walk, but not very far in case the church bells ring. I wish Daddy and Harold and Gordon could come too.

Journal

Auntie Grace is back from the hospital and seems to be getting well quickly, so last weekend, when Daddy came, Mummy went home with him.

Uncle Bill's been very busy for the last few weeks, even though every evening on his way home he went to visit Auntie Grace. He'd have supper as soon as he was home and then go straight out to the back garden, where he's building an air raid shelter. We go to bed soon after supper, but on Saturdays we watch and sometimes can help. It's bad when it rains because the shelter's not ready for a roof yet, so it gets very muddy, and it's hard to dig. Uncle Bill is working ever so hard, shoveling and shoveling. He told us, "This has to be six feet deep at least, and I won't be able to stand up in it."

When he wants something from the house, he says, "Margaret, please go in and ask Auntie Grace for my yardstick," or "Can you fetch my hammer, please, and the nails I put out on the table," and sometimes, "Richard, can you help me carry one of those long pieces of wood from the pile? I'm going to have to shore up this wall before I dig any more." Of course, Richard couldn't be much help carrying a plank, but Uncle Bill made it seem as though he was. Luckily, he has a friend who sometimes helps, too, on Saturdays. Lots of people are building shelters because everyone seems to think the Germans will start air raids soon and will probably bomb the large oil refineries that aren't far from here.

*   *   *

Here I am again. I wrote that a while ago. Luckily, Uncle Bill has finished the air raid shelter because last night I suddenly felt someone shaking me and saying, "Margaret, Margaret, wake up, dear." "Oh," trying to bury myself under the bedclothes with my eyes tight shut, "Oh, did we oversleep? It can't be morning yet!" "No, but you must get up. Now! Quickly! The siren just sounded, so we have to go down to the shelter. Get up and wake Richard. You must both dress. It's chilly out there." I jumped out of bed, awake now, and leaned over Richard's bed to wake him. He grunted and rubbed his eyes and, finally, had his feet on the floor, so I turned around to dress, expecting him to, too. Luckily, I turned back to make sure. He was trying to put his arm through a leg of his shorts, so I had to sort him out and help him into the rest of his clothes. "Children, come, come on. Hurry!" Auntie Grace called from the bottom of the stairs. We stumbled down somehow and followed her outside and down the ladder into the shelter. We could hear planes close by and a few thuds as bombs hit the ground or a refinery. I don't remember much more, for almost as soon as we were settled into the garden chairs Uncle Bill had set up, we went off to sleep again. They must have carried us back up to bed when the raid was over because we woke up there with our clothes on. We were late to school, but so was everyone else.

The good thing for us about the raids was that the

next weekend, when Mummy and Daddy came, Mummy said, "This is ridiculous! You're where the bombs are, and we're not having any! Never mind about school. We'll take you home with us," and she meant right away! We scurried around finding all our things: clothes, books, toys, and one or two photos Auntie Grace had taken of us and stuffed it all in the boot of the car. Richard and I were as excited and eager to go as puppies are to go for a walk. Still, we were sad to say, "Goodbye," to Auntie Grace and Uncle Bill and had big hugs, promising, "We'll write," and, "We'll come and see you as soon as possible."

We expected to be home in no time, but the journey took ages, and Mummy suggested we should take turns telling what we most wanted to find again at home. Richard said, "More of my soldiers," and I said, "Bob," (our dog) because suddenly I realized how much I'd missed him. "Meccano, my doll's pram, Harold and Gordon, (but they won't be home until the summer holidays), the grandfather clock, the gong, I want to ring it for tea this afternoon." On and on, until finally we were pulling up to the curb and scrambled out of the car. Mummy came quickly to unlock the front door. Then we were in the hall, but it was funny: everything looked smaller than I remembered. I suppose because I'm bigger.

Handen Road
September, 1940

Journal

It had been lovely being home. The best part was not having to say goodbye to Mummy and Daddy after the weekends that they came to Ulcombe. Breakfast was the same, dinner was the same, bedtime was the same. It felt so safe. Then having Harold and Gordon home for their summer holidays was special. When France fell, Hitler said that the Germans would soon have crossed the channel, and he would be sitting in Buckingham Palace by August 15th. But he wasn't, and Daddy took us all up to see Buckingham Palace without Hitler in it. There were lots of people there, all of us gloating.

Now, though, terrible things are happening. Late in August the Germans torpedoed a ship taking child evacuees to Canada, and hardly any of them survived. Then, because he couldn't cross the channel, Hitler has begun the Blitz. He's determined to occupy England as well as the continent. It's awful. Every night, and some days, there are air raids. Often they go on for the whole night in spite of all the Spitfires can do. We spend most nights in the cellar. The Woolwich docks are only two miles away. Blackheath, which is covered with anti-aircraft guns, and so also a target, even if a dangerous one, is nearer still. Our cellar is small. There's no room for beds. The safest place in it is supposed to be the coke hole because it's under three flights of stairs. So that's where Richard and I sleep, on cushions on top of the coke. (Not the drink, but fuel that comes from coal and is used in closed stoves and to bank up fires at night.) It is not at all comfortable, but we can lie down, while the others have to sit up all night. We always have to go down to "bed" long before they come. Mummy leaves the light on for us, but it's still not a pleasant place. Sometimes Harold, who had infantile-paralysis when he was nine and has a crippled leg, which makes him limp, after we've gone to bed alone down there, limps back and forth, back and forth above the cellar. That makes us more afraid than the air raids do. Then everyone is down there with us. Even though it's more dangerous (the bombing there is worse than here), Daddy goes to the city nearly every day. Hitler is still not sitting in Buckingham Palace though!

Quite often the air raid warning goes off here, and we have to be in the cellar during the day. We play games, sometimes board games like draughts (checkers), sometimes guessing games like I Spy. Gordon taught me to play cribbage, and we played it so often that I know without thinking which numbers add up to fifteen. Now that Harold and Gordon have gone back to Tumbridge Wells, I sometimes write in this journal. I've just written this down in the cellar. Every night now there is an air raid and often nearly all day too. We all spend the night in the cellar. Richard and I go to bed down there early. Mummy and Daddy (and Harold and Gordon before they went back to Tonbridge Wells) only come down as soon as the bombing seems close. Often they sit up most of the night because the cellar's so small there's no room for beds. The day the Germans bombed the docks at Woolwich with incendiary bombs, Mummy and Richard and I were down there nearly all day. Daddy was in the city. They did it so that they could come back at night and see, by the light of the burning buildings, what else to bomb. The docks are about two miles from us, so when the all clear went, late in the afternoon, we came up from the cellar and saw the sky all red and orange like a brilliant sunset, only it was in the East. Sure enough the German planes came back and bombed all night long.

Next day

Journal

There weren't any raids the next day, which was a relief, but there certainly were at night.

Now, we are in Northampton which is roughly fifty miles north of London. The raids kept on, some very close because the big marshalling yard at Hither Green is a target for bombers. So, after a few more really scary nights Daddy said, "We must get out of London. We have to leave here even if we only drive to the Chiselhurst caves. The trouble is lots of people are going there, so we might have to spend whole nights in the car." He thought for a moment. "Hmm, wait. I do have some relatives in Northampton. We haven't seen each other for a long time, but I'm sure they will help us. Hurry! We must pack."

We scurried around, packing a few clothes, closed up the house and collected Grandma on the way. Richard and I knew we were leaving again . . . and again didn't know anything about where we were going, but it didn't feel nearly as bad because we were with Mummy and Daddy. He somehow rented a van to take us to Euston. We huddled in the back, seeing nothing until we arrived and scrambled out. It was pretty stinky there, with crowds of people all pushing and jostling to get through the barriers. Then, somehow, we lost Richard. We were all terribly worried, frantic really, not daring to split up to

31

look for him in case we lost each other, too. Oh, what a relief when there he was, right in front of us, tears running down his cheeks, of course even more upset than we'd been. He hugged Mummy and me, saying through his sobs, "Where were you? I called out lots of times, but no one answered, and people kept pushing me all over the place." He buried his face in Mummy's coat as though he would never let go.

After that Mummy and I each held one of his hands while Daddy and Grandma waited in line to buy tickets. That took ages as the line in front of them hardly seemed to grow any shorter. We were all very tired of being jostled around, but at last we were through the barrier and on the train. Then that didn't start for ages, and we hadn't been going for long before there was an air raid warning. The train stopped. We pulled down all the blinds in case the windows were broken and were ready to lie on the floor if we heard bombs. Since the carriage was packed, goodness knows how squashed we'd have been. Some of us under the seats probably.

Fortunately, we soon started off again and reached Northampton in about an hour. We found a taxi to take us to Daddy's relatives' house, and the five of us stood at Auntie Katie's doorstep hoping and hoping they could take us in. They don't have a telephone, and we left home in such a hurry that we couldn't find any other way to let them know. I'll always remember Auntie Katie's face when she opened the door and saw us all so tired and worried. It went quickly from looking shocked to looking very kind, as we've found it usually does. Daddy said, "Hello, Katie. We didn't know where to go."

At once she said, "Jamie! Oh, Jamie." then, "My ducks. Oh, my ducks! Come in, come in my ducks."

They were all wonderful. It's a really little house, the kind that opens right onto the street and only has a tiny backyard where the loo is, but after Auntie Katie had given us tea and something to eat, she set about organizing where we could sleep. There wasn't room for us all here, but she said to Daddy, "Annie and Fred are only just around the corner. I'm sure they'll manage something. Wait a few minutes and I'll go round and ask them. I know you must all be desperately tired." She went right away and was back in no time. They would find some kind of beds for Grandma and Richard and me. That's where we've been sleeping. Grandma has a camp bed, Richard a sort of reclining chair in which he manages to sleep very well, and their daughter, Mary, who's a grown up, is sharing her bed with me. They're all very kind. Both families moved stuff around in their houses to make room for us. Everybody's pretty cramped, but for us it's much better than the cellar! They are somehow managing to find food for us as well. I think Mummy brought our ration books, but it still must be difficult.

Each day we go looking for a house we can rent, but there are other people doing this, and we're not having any luck. I heard Auntie Katie say to Mummy, "Well, I've been wondering. My youngest sister, Olive, lives on a farm about six miles away. Perhaps they could have you. Olive isn't always the easiest person to live with, but I'd say it's certainly worth a try. They have a big farmhouse."

Tomorrow we're going to see them. Probably Grandma won't come. I think she's getting homesick for her little flat, even though she knows it's dangerous there. Yes, she says I'm right. She wants to go home.

Home Farm
Gayton, Northampton
October, 1940

Journal

We went to see Auntie Katie's sister Olive and her husband, at their farm in Gayton, a little village about six miles from Northampton, the day after Auntie Katie suggested we should, and we're here! They were very welcoming and said, "Of course you must stay here," and we're here! Then, in a few days, they agreed that an old man, a friend and client of Daddy's, should come there too, with his sister-in-law, who takes care of him. That meant a major reshuffling of bedrooms to fit us all in. Uncle Aubrey and Auntie Olive, Richard and I started calling them that right away, moved into the smaller bedroom across the hall, which was really Mary's. She's their little girl, and is only three with lots of curly hair, which is always full of tangles in the morning, but she is very patient while they're being brushed out. The three of them are sharing that room, while Mummy and Daddy and Richard and I are sharing their room. Mr. Manning has what had been the spare room and his sister-in-law has what used to be Mary's playroom. It's a lot of people to fit in after there only being three of them, and none of us has any idea how long it will be for. I like our room, because as well as a window at the front of the house, there's a little one on the side that looks over the farmyard. We can see chickens scrabbling around and, sometimes, one of the farm workers leading the horses in or out. The horses make a clopping noise on the cobbles, so we know when to look.

We all love this house. It's built of stone. Over the front door, the date when it was built (1720) is carved in the "lintel"; I think Daddy called it that. Anyhow, it's the big oblong stone across the top of the door. The walls are really thick, so you can climb up and sit right in the window even though they aren't real window seats, just really wide ledges. I love doing that, either to read or just watch what's going on outside.

Folded against the walls there are shutters. These have to be closed every night. There's blackout here, too, all over the country in fact. We're not allowed to show even the slightest gleam. Sometimes, after dark, the local policeman cycles round the village to make sure everyone's blackout is perfect. The few cars and bikes have things like metal eyelids over their lights to make them shine down. Except on moonlit nights, it's pitch black outside. Because the lights only shine a few feet ahead, cars must go very slowly. It's pretty much like driving in a pea-souper,[*] a thick, greenish yellow fog that often came in the autumn and winter.

Here it's only the blackout that makes it seem as though there's a war on, except, of course, that everyone listens to the news bulletins and hears all the awful things that are happening with the bombing in London,

---

[*]Mostly coal and coke were used for heating, and the smoke they emitted turned mist into dense fog.

and worse, with the Germans all over Europe. Of course there's a shortage of some kinds of food, and we're promised that will get worse because so much has to come from overseas. But on a farm there's always a little something extra, like a few eggs. They're, oh so good: absolutely fresh. I think I'd like to live here always. At least I feel that way on the weekends, but I don't like it when Daddy goes up to London for three or four days during the week, and I know Mummy worries about him. There is still a lot of bombing. She worries about Grandma, too, now that she has gone back to her flat, but she was determined to go.

Even here, with fresh eggs available, we feel the effects of rationing. If we say we're still hungry when everything on the table is gone, Mummy says, "Dame Henrietta" (someone or other) "said you should always leave the table feeling you could eat a little more." We often do, but for people who aren't living on a farm, or don't have good vegetable gardens, it must be worse. There are gardens in all kinds of unusual places, like the verges of even busy roads, and railway embankments, sometimes even the railway platforms.

Now I must go and lay the table for dinner. I can smell it cooking: rabbit pie. Uncle Aubrey went out with his gun this morning and came back with two rabbits. Before the war I would have hated the idea of eating rabbits, but now I'm glad to. They really are good, and perhaps with two of them there'll be a little more than when we just have rationed meat.

Journal

It wasn't long after we came to Gayton that we started school. Mummy took us on the first school day after we arrived. It's even closer than Manor Lane was but much smaller. There are only two classrooms, and all the children fit in easily. The youngest ones, from five to nine, are in the small room and the older ones in the big room with the head teacher. Her name is Miss Bamford. She's stout and pale with grey hair, pulled back tight, and rimless glasses. We had to go into the big room for her to decide what standard we'd be in. Richard isn't old enough to be in a standard yet, so it was obvious he'd be with the little ones, but nobody seemed sure about me. I thought I'd finished Standard 1 while we were in Ulcombe, but Miss Bamford asked me some arithmetic questions I couldn't answer. I think it was because I was nervous in front of all those big children and, too, because it was several weeks since we'd been in school.

Anyhow, Miss Bamford decided I should be in Standard 1, which is the top one in the little ones' room. At first I felt rather indignant because I didn't think I'd been given a fair chance to show what I could do, but I was soon very glad not to be in Miss Bamford's room. She is well named. There's a cane on top of her desk which she uses a lot, BAM . . . BAM . . . BAM. Miss McKinley isn't at all like that. She's very quiet and kind and manages all the different levels, from children who haven't learned to read yet to my class. We read a lot, history and geography as well as story books. Because I like reading, I'm glad to be back in school. We couldn't bring books with us, but the school has some I can borrow, and Miss McKinley says there's a library van that comes around every other week and has a lot more.

There's a boy in Standard 1 with me who likes to read too, and we tell each other about books we've enjoyed. We sit next to each other in a desk made for two, two lids under which we keep our books, papers, pens and pencils, and two inkwells, but one long seat. It's funny: his name is Colin West, and there's another boy, in Richard's class, whose name is Michael East. Both their fathers are farmers, so perhaps the names come from where the farms are. I know Colin and Michael's grandfathers were farmers, too, and probably their great grandfathers. Who knows how far back! There are quite a lot of children who have the same surnames because there are several brothers and sisters, of course, but also cousins. There probably aren't more than ten or so different names in the whole school. Just the other day, though, two more evacuees came into our room, and they have a different name from anybody's. Well, so do we, even though our name is Jones!

Sometimes the Rector comes to see how much we are learning. He looks at us over the top of his glasses and mostly only asks us about scripture, a subject we have every day. Mummy says that's because it's a church school. We did some scripture at Manor Lane and Ulcombe, too, but not every day, as we do now, and nobody came to ask us questions. The Rector doesn't stay very long with our class but spends longer in the big room and probably asks more questions there. It's always very quiet. I expect they're all scared of what Miss Bamford will do when he's gone if they play around. We see him in church every Sunday, but although there aren't many people there, he doesn't know our names yet. He must have been picking walnuts last Saturday from the tree in his garden. On Sunday, during the sermon, he held his hands up, palms towards the congregation, to show how people in India give greetings. They were all brown with walnut stain. It made them look like an Indian's hands. Daddy was shaking with laughter he was trying not to let out. Mummy told me a new word (suppress) when she was helping me go over this. It means keep under control. That's what Daddy was doing, trying to suppress his laughter, but he wasn't too successful.

We have made some new friends who don't go to Gayton School but to schools in Northampton. Their names are Elizabeth (who's three years older than me) and Michael (who's a fortnight older). They live just up the road from us and are fun. We spend lots of time at their house or, more often, out in their garden or their yard. There's a big barn in the yard and a pigsty. They're thinking of getting a piglet to raise because then they'd have more meat and some really good bacon.

Uncle Aubrey has pigs at Home Farm, and one of them is always for the family, so that helps eke out the meat ration, which is very small. We save any scraps we have left and all the outside leaves from lettuces and cabbages. Pigs will eat just about anything and enjoy it!

Journal

We're very lucky. Everyone here gets along really well and seems to enjoy each other's company. The only thing is: I know Mummy worries about Daddy when he goes up to London every week. She manages not to seem worried to us, but sometimes I hear her say something to Auntie Olive that makes me know.

There are still lots of bombing raids on London. One weekend the church right next door to our house was bombed with incendiary bombs that burned most of the building. The next weekend high explosives were dropped there, right next to us, and finished the job! Now the Greensmiths, who live just across the road, have invited Daddy to stay with them whenever he's in London, which is the middle of every week. Their house is no safer, but at least he's not alone.[*]

[*]I didn't think about this during the war and probably not for a long time afterwards. Since then, though, I've read a lot and seen movies of things that happened in WWI, and I have some idea of what it must have felt like for people to be in the midst of another war, especially for those who had been in battles or had anyone they loved in them, which was most of the population. My father fought in WWI in some of the biggest battles. He had a medal for bravery for going behind enemy lines to bring back information. Also he had some quite bad injuries. It must have been awful for him, and the millions like him, to know what being in battle was like, and for many to sit in London, as he did night after night, with bombs raining down around them.

Christmas here was great fun. Daddy stayed for longer, and Harold and Gordon came for their school holidays, about three weeks. Because there wasn't even the tiniest space in a bedroom for them at Home Farm, they slept at Uncle Aubrey's mother and father's house, but they had all their meals with us. There were eleven of us at each meal. Richard and Mary and I had to sit at a little table because there wasn't room for us all around the big one.

Christmas dinner was wonderful, even though the turkey, which Daddy managed to get in London and bring with him on the train, turned out to be going bad. It was lucky for us that we were on a farm. Uncle Aubrey just had to go to the rick yard and get three chickens instead. We had them with stuffing and roast potatoes, bread sauce, brussel sprouts and carrots from the garden, with delicious gravy. It didn't seem as though there was any kind of rationing. Auntie Olive and Mummy had also managed to find the ingredients for Christmas pudding. Auntie Olive poured brandy over it and made it flame. Something we had never seen done before.

I think we all felt lucky to be with the people we loved and to be able to have such a festive meal. Everybody seemed to be enjoying themselves, as though we had forgotten the war for a little while.

Journal

It's snowing hard, so we're all indoors. There are bad things and good things to write about. When I think about it, I'm fairly sure some of the good things happened because of the bad things, so I'll start with the bad ones.

In 1939, when the war began, every one seemed sure it would be over before Christmas. Well, obviously it isn't. We've just had another Christmas, and the Germans are still bombing London. A couple of Sunday nights ago they bombed the city, all round St. Paul's, with incendiary bombs. When Daddy came back at the end of the next week he said, "It was horrendous. People are calling it the Second Fire of London. I was so glad you were here!" Not long ago they bombed Coventry and destroyed the cathedral there as well as some factories that made munitions and some that made aeroplanes, which we need lots of. Since then they've bombed several other cities, including Birmingham, which isn't far from here. Then we keep hearing about ships being sunk, the army in North Africa isn't doing well at all, and added to all that, the Germans are still threatening to invade. That seemed especially serious when the whole village was told what to do if the church bell rang.

We're all to go down the hill to the railway tunnel,

which is a long one. There are only about three hundred people in Gayton, even with evacuees, so it wouldn't be nearly as crowded as the London Underground stations are. Everyone must take their identity card and ration book, though who knows what use they'd be in the tunnel, let alone if the Germans were all over the place! The grownups laughed when it was announced that any one unable to walk there would be taken down on the bier, because Mr. Manning would have to be. They were all laughing because they know how much he enjoys his couple of glasses of beer at the Queen Victoria each morning. Daddy had to explain to Richard and me that this was a pun, and then we laughed too.

I said that there were some good things. There were a lot. I think people tried very hard to make it a happy time in spite of all the horrors. The first good thing, and certainly a happy one, was that Daddy organized carol singing for any grownups who'd like to do it. There were quite a few, and for a couple of evenings before they went caroling, they came here to practice. The piano is in the lounge, right under our bedroom, so Richard and I would go to sleep to the sound of carols. I loved it when they sang "While shepherds watched their flocks by night." I like the tune, but also there are shepherds in Gayton, which makes it seem special.

Other really good things, which happened after Christmas, were the children's parties. There were five. One family gave two: one for children around Richard's and my ages, one for teenagers like Harold and Gordon. The best one was at the Roes'. Perhaps that's why it seemed best. We know them best, and it was first. Besides that, Mrs. Roe, of all the hostesses, seemed to really enjoy it herself and knew lots of good games. The one Richard and I didn't know before, though I think Harold and Gordon did, was "Murder."

First, Mrs. Roe passed out enough cards for each of us to have one. Nobody was to tell what their card was, except the person who had a king. That person would be the detective and would stay behind in the lounge, while everybody else went all around the completely dark house, feeling their way and often bumping into each other. This was kind of scary, but we all knew each other, so it wasn't really scary. After a little milling around like this, someone, who had the only Jack given out, would whisper to their victim, "You're dead," or perhaps they'd do a gentle squeeze, not quite a throttle. The victim was to count to ten, while the murderer scurried away as fast as possible, and then scream. That was the signal for everyone to stop exactly where they were. All the lights were turned back on, and the detective came out to find the body and see where everyone was. Then we all gathered in the lounge again for the detective to ask all sorts of questions, trying to discover who was the murderer; everyone but the murderer had to tell the truth. We played three times, and by the third one we all knew what we were doing. When we played at the Roes,' no one tried any silly tricks, though once or twice that happened at other parties. It was a sort of scary game but fun, a different scary than air raids. It's funny really that we didn't mind playing Murder in the pitch dark, but it had been pitch dark walking up the road and then just wonderful when we went into the Roes' brightly lit house. It was as though we were like the shepherds when the angels spread light all around them.

After Murder and a few more games, we had delicious refreshments. Every party we went to managed this somehow, even though no one could have had much food to spare. People must have saved up from their rations for a few weeks and set stuff aside that wasn't rationed but was hard to come by. Everywhere we went, as well as the bright lights after our dark walk, there were scrumptious smells.

The party here at Home Farm was really good, and it was the best house for Murder because there are two sets of stairs, and a murderer could commit the crime on one set and speedily make it to the other. The grownups knew Mary might be scared, so Mummy and Auntie Olive asked Richard to hold hands with her and be sure not to let go. Actually, I think he rather liked looking after her instead of being the one looked after. We also had delicious food here. Auntie Olive is a very good cook and, of course, Mummy, who is too, helped a lot. They could use fresh eggs for egg salad sandwiches, which most other people couldn't, and they made wonderful sausage rolls, with sausage meat Auntie Olive had made when Uncle Aubrey slaughtered a pig.

Lunch is ready, and it's hardly snowing anymore. We'll probably go tobogganing this afternoon. One of Uncle Aubrey's fields should be really good for it. He thinks he can find us a toboggan,[*] and the Roes have two or three, so no one will have to wait too long for a turn. Yes, we did go. I think all the children in the village were there. It was tremendous fun, with lots of shouting: "Race you," "Hey, out of my way," "Did you see that?" But it was bitterly cold and, of course, I was wearing a skirt. The wind blew all the way up my legs. When I came home, before the others, they were blue. Mummy said, "Oh, You poor darling. I know what we'll do. You can wear a pair of

[*]This is not like a toboggan in the U.S. It is what is called there a sled.

45

Richard's shorts." She went to fetch them while I sat near the kitchen fire and warmed up. They made a tremendous difference. Of course, I still had bare knees, but the wind didn't blow *all* the way up my legs.

Richard and I started back first, when we thought it was time for tea. We were certainly hungry enough for it! Pretty soon Gordon came in saying, "Harold's having a few more goes. The snow's really fast now. It's packed down, and there aren't as many people getting in the way."

Not much later, as it was beginning to get dark, in came Harold, with blood dripping from his ear and a woe-begone expression. "I was swooping down the hill going wonderfully fast, but at the bottom I couldn't stop. I really needed to stick out my legs, and put my feet down on the ice, but I couldn't do that. I tried, but my legs said, "No," and I went sailing through the hedge, right where it's all hawthorn bushes. Ouch!" This was to Mummy, who was rinsing the blood away.

"It's not too bad. It just needs a couple of bits of elastoplast, and you'll be as good as new," she said as she finished swabbing the blood away.

"He's lucky," I thought. I knew what that hedge was like because one day Michael Roe and I had tried to take a short cut through it and found it completely impossible. If he hadn't been going so fast, Harold could still have been stuck in it.

I must stop now and hope we can go tobogganing again tomorrow.

Journal

The news hasn't been good at all. Everybody here listens to it on the wireless, but it's dismal and mostly, when it's over, we're all quiet for a few minutes. There's still a lot of bombing and still a chance of invasion. Sometimes when someone has left the paper in a room I'm in alone, I read the front page, but it makes me feel awful. There are terrible stories about what the Germans are doing to Jewish people, and there are sometimes stories about evacuees being badly treated. Richard and I were very lucky to be with the Turners, but Harold and Gordon weren't at all happy at their first billet, and the second one isn't much better. They don't talk about it much when they're here, but their letters show how miserable they sometimes are. One good thing is that, instead of playing rugger or cricket, which he doesn't much enjoy, Gordon is allowed to have an allotment and grow vegetables. He loves doing that. Another good thing is that Tunbridge Wells is never bombed. They'll come here for the Easter holidays, so that will be good. I love it when they're here.

There isn't any bombing here either, but last night, Uncle Aubrey was on fire-watching duty, and there was a bomb. Fortunately, it fell in a field. Not many people, including us, even knew about it until the morning. Uncle

Aubrey and Charlie Munton, the other fire-watcher, heard a thud. When they went out to look, they could see flames lighting up the sky above the Bugbrooke Road. Uncle Aubrey told us about it when he came in from milking. They had set off at once and managed to get to where the bomb was in just a few minutes. There wasn't going to be any damage. "Luckily," he said, "the bomb fell into a shallow pit in the middle of a field where mangel-wursels[*] had just been harvested. We'd carried some large cans of water, but that was soon used up, and the bomb was still alight. There wasn't any other water near by, so I started picking up handfuls of earth and throwing them onto it. Charlie soon joined in, shouting with every handful he threw, 'Toik thaat, toik thaat!' and we soon had it out."

While he had us laughing, Uncle Aubrey told us a bit more about Charlie Munton. He has bowed legs. Quite a lot of the villagers have. Auntie Olive says it's because when they were children their families couldn't afford good food. Uncle Aubrey says, "Charlie Munton couldn't stop a pig in a passage." Then he went on to tell us how Charlie would try to win at darts in the pub, where the fire-watchers spend the night. Each person playing is supposed to stand with his heels against a line. To be as close to the board as possible, Charlie Munton wears boots two sizes too big and makes sure his toes are right up in the toes of the boots.

There's another story we like to hear Uncle Aubrey tell. This one is about his shepherd, Jack George. As Jack George was driving a few sheep from one field to another,

---

[*]Mangel-wursels are very large beets that look like yellow turnips or, to English people, swedes. They are only used to feed animals.

a car pulled up close to him, and the driver said, "George, can you tell me the way to Tiffield?" Jack George knew the way to Tiffield as well as he knew the way to his own back door, but he growled, "Ow jer know my name was Jarge?" "Guessed it." "Roit then, you guess the way to Tiffle."

I'd already heard this story when Elizabeth and I did something like it. Ever since the threat of invasion, all the sign posts have had their signs removed. Now there are just the posts with no signs. We have been warned many times over the wireless that we should on no account give directions to anybody we don't know. One Saturday morning when Elizabeth and I were walking up the same road as Jack George had been on, a big, expensive looking car pulled up close to us. The driver rolled down his window and said, "Hello, can you tell me the way to Eastcote?" In that car it would have taken very little time to get there, but we weren't supposed to give directions. We gave totally wrong ones instead that would take him to a gated road where he'd have to get out to open the gate. There was a sign that said, "Close the gate after you." So he'd have to get out of the car and back into it twice because he'd have to do that all over again when he reached the other end of the field. Once he'd done that, he'd be close to Tiffield but not any closer to Eastcote. He hadn't sounded like anyone from around Northampton, so we felt quite proud of ourselves for misleading him. After all he could have been a German spy.

There's just time to tell one more of Uncle Aubrey's stories. It's about a wonderful old woman, Miss Webber, who lives in a cottage on the road Elizabeth and I were on when we gave the wrong directions. She manages to do everything for herself, even going to the pump farther up the road for her water, pumping it and carrying it back.

On Mondays, the days just about everyone does their washing, she must have to go to the pump two or three times. Uncle Aubrey says Miss Webber is very proud of her age and will gladly tell anyone who asks, "I'll be eighty-two coom next moock spreadin' time," and if it happens that the fields will soon be spread with manure, she's likely to say, "I'll be eighty-three coom mooc spreadin' time after next." This way she adds a good year to her age, but she does have every right to be proud of it!

Now I must do some homework before it's too late. I have to write a composition about a giant, and I don't know how to begin. Perhaps I could write about Miss Webber. In a way she's a giant.

Journal

We often have bad news about ships in the Atlantic Ocean. Not long ago lots of Merchant Marine ships bringing food were sunk, which means there's stricter rationing. We're very lucky to be on a farm. I think perhaps we'd be really hungry if Uncle Aubrey didn't sometimes kill a pig and sometimes shoot rabbits and pigeons. I'd never have thought so, but pigeon pie is really good. There's a shortage of fruit and vegetables too, but he's made a vegetable garden from a big part of the lawn. There are just beginning to be delicious early vegetables, like radishes and spring onions, spinach, too, but I don't much like that; it makes my mouth feel funny, sort of puckered up.

When the boys were here for Easter, Auntie Olive told us where she thought there would be some wild watercress, "It's in the field a little way past Chain Walk and opposite the Britain cottages. You'll fine the stream easily; after the rain it'll be running fast. You'd better wear your Wellington boots because you'll have to wade in." We went with Gordon, who found the stream easily and could wade in further than Richard and I could because his boots were much higher. We picked a lot of watercress, but Richard and I became bolder and bolder, so we had a lot of water in our boots because we didn't realize the

51

stream was deeper in some places. It didn't really matter. Everyone was delighted with the watercress, and Mummy stuffed our boots with old newspaper, so they were dry by the next morning.

One good thing has happened. I mean something that affects everybody, not just us. It came from something awful though. Last month there was a huge air raid on London that did lots of damage and killed a lot of people. When Daddy came back, he said, "The city looks awful. Many of the buildings have been completely destroyed. Fortunately, although it was hit, St. Paul's wasn't too badly damaged. In the West End, Westminster Abbey wasn't so lucky, nor were the Houses of Parliament." What's good about it, though, is that since then there haven't been any more raids on London. The Germans are now bombing cities north of here; not so good really.

A while ago I realized how worried Mummy must have been when Daddy went off to his office in the city. I was in our bedroom one morning when Mummy and Auntie Olive were making the beds. As they did Mummy puffed up a pillow and put it down lengthwise on Daddy's side saying, "That's Jamie." Just about always he goes for three days. On Thursdays he comes back with his attaché case full of work to do on Fridays and Mondays. Auntie Olive has cleared out a little room, which was mostly for storage, and now it's his Gayton office. Occasionally Mummy goes to London with him for the day. He goes to his office, and she goes to Lee. She said once, "Every time I walk from the station, I think, as I get near Handen Road, "Is our house still there?"

Journal

We are all glad that there haven't been any raids for more than a fortnight. I think Mummy's the gladdest of all.

It's a pity Harold and Gordon aren't here now. They'd love what we are doing. It's haymaking time. Because the weather's just right, all the farmers are haymaking. A few days ago, they cut down the tall grass in the hay fields with scythes, and every day it has been dry and warm, so now there's hay. The men work very hard for very long days in case the weather changes. If it rains before the hay has been brought in, they have to wait for it to dry again or it's ruined. We have double daylight saving time now. That's to give farmers, who have fewer workmen because some are off to the war, longer daylight hours for harvesting. They work until ten o'clock, when it's almost dark. What makes it so good for us is that at five o'clock the workmen's whole families take tea to them and have tea with them. It's a very happy time. There's one big tree in the field they're working in now, which provides plenty of shade for five or six families.

Auntie Olive and Mummy make several thermoses of tea and several kinds of sandwiches, sometimes egg, almost always cucumber, occasionally cheese, if there is still enough of the ration. I think though that Auntie Olive knew from other years that she'd have to set some aside, at least for Uncle Aubrey. He'll be working until it's too dark to do any more. Often there are paste sandwiches too. Although we all sit on the ground in family groups, there's a lot of conversation and joking from one to another, and little children run back and forth, especially when another group has cousins or an aunt or uncle or grandmother in it. That's often.

As soon as the men have finished eating, they're back to work. Then the children start playing games together, like tag, or the little ones will play "Ring Around the Roses" laughing when they "all fall down." All the time the older children are watching for when the next wagonload is ready to go to the rick yard full of hay. Sometimes a few of us are allowed to ride on top of the load. The wagon may be pulled either by one of the cart horses or by the tractor. There's only one tractor (Uncle Aubrey hasn't been able to buy another because of the war), so there are six horses. I like riding on the hay when the wagon's pulled by a cart horse because the tractor smells of petrol, and the horse, usually, at least from the top of the load of hay, doesn't smell at all. From the top of the load, you can see into some of the gardens that you can't see from the roadway. Usually there are vegetables growing, and almost always there are roses climbing on an arch or up a wall. As we went by, from high up on the hay we could see into Miss Webber's garden, where she has vegetables and lots of flowers.

Absolutely the best thing about haymaking is the delicious smell of the hay. I think it's my favourite of all smells, even better than violets or roses.

Journal

After the Easter Holidays I started at another school, and I have homework now, so I can't write in this journal very often. In March, Miss Mackinley, with some kind of warning in her voice, said, "Margaret, I think you're ready to go into Miss Bamford's room after the holidays." I didn't like that idea at all. Nobody likes her, and she's very quick to use her cane. When I came home and told Mummy, she was worried about it too, and Auntie Olive, who had been the head teacher before Miss Bamford and knew what things were like in her classroom, said I'd definitely be better off somewhere else. The very next morning Mummy went into Northampton to see Miss Marston, the headmistress of the High School, where my friend Elizabeth goes. Miss Marston said I'd have to go in for a test. That was arranged for the next morning, so Mummy took me in on the early bus. The teacher of the class with girls of my age gave me a test in English and arithmetic, and asked me a few questions about what I like to read. Then we saw Miss Marston, who told us she'd send a letter in a day or two.

At last her letter came. It took Mummy longer than I'd have thought it would to read it. Was that good or bad? I wondered, then realized it wouldn't take that long if it only said "No." Finally, after what seemed like a week of Sundays, Mummy said, "Yes, they'll have you, but unfortunately there isn't room for anyone else in the Upper Second, which is where you should be. Miss Marston says you can go into the Lower Third for this term but start next year in next year's Lower Third. You're sure to find this term really difficult, but it will be better than being in Miss Bamford's room.

The first thing to do was walk up the road to ask Elizabeth if she'd help me on my first day, the day after tomorrow. Before I could actually go, I had to have the school uniform. Mummy and I went into Northampton again to buy it for the summer term: two green dresses, a blazer, a raincoat and a panama hat. This meant a lot of clothing coupons, and probably Mummy used some of hers. We bought a satchel, too, because I was going to have homework.

Now I was all ready, and the next morning, after I'd kissed Mummy and Auntie Olive goodbye, I walked up to the Roes' house with the money for the bus fare in the shoulder purse Auntie Grace and Uncle Bill gave me. My new pencil case was in my satchel on my back with plimsolls I had to have for gym. Elizabeth was waiting for me, and we set off for the first bus of the day. There weren't many other passengers until Blizworth, when lots got on and more still at Milton, the last stop on the way. The bus was jammed with passengers, lots of them standing in the aisle, so Elizabeth and I gave up our seats, as our parents had told us we must always do for grownups. It wasn't far now, and I was beginning to be scared. All too soon for me we reached the bus station and hurried out to the street. It seemed a very short stone's throw to the school. The butterflies in my stomach were fluttering. In the cloakroom, among lots of jabbering girls, Elizabeth showed me where to hang my things, took me along to the Lower Third's classroom and was gone. There was lots of jabbering there, too. Then suddenly it was absolutely quiet. Miss James, the teacher, introduced me and found me a seat. I was to share a double desk with a girl named Jennifer.

Just as I'd left in the morning, Mummy had said, "I'm afraid most of the work will be hard for you. After all, these girls are at least a year older than you, but don't worry, the teacher knows that, and she'll help you, I'm sure." She was right. Miss James was very helpful, and when I felt really stupid, I only had to remember that I might have been at Gayton School with Miss Bamford. Then I felt much better! Luckily, it was Wednesday, when the whole school has a half-holiday. After the last bell, Elizabeth came for me, and we went home together. I soon felt all right going home alone on the bus, which was good because I have another half holiday that she doesn't have.

Oh, but I was very glad a week later that we went on the bus together each morning. The army is doing manoeuvres all around Gayton with two teams, one is us, the other the Germans. There are men in uniform all over the village and in the fields around us (which doesn't please Uncle Aubrey much). Of course, they only have British uniforms, so they wear different caps to be able to recognize which side is which; only, we don't know. Yesterday morning, the bus was just a little way out of the village when it stopped. The driver called out, "Darn it. The road's blocked," and everyone worried about being late for work or school. There was a sudden banging on the door, so the driver had to open it. A soldier in a black beret and with a gun in his hand, came up the steps shouting, "Everybody, stay where you are. One of the enemy has crossed our lines. We have to search the bus." He walked slowly to the back, staring at each of us and looking under every seat, with his gun all the time a threat. Thank goodness it was very quick. He didn't find anyone and soon was off the bus and shouting orders for the barricade to be removed. As we started again, everyone gave a huge sigh of relief. We all knew this was part of the manoeuvres, but it felt horribly real, and no one said much until we reached Blizworth. We were all thinking, "Supposing we had been invaded; the bus would have been searched by an armed German." Then suddenly everyone was talking at once, some to the Blizworth people, some to each other. Elizabeth and I said simultaneously, "Phew!"

The manoeuvres ended on Saturday and on Sunday morning, both sides came to church. The regular church-goers, including us and the Roes, knew that we'd better be there early, or all the pews would be filled. When we reached the church porch, we were met by Mrs. Browne, the rector's by no-means-popular wife. We'd only seen her in church twice since we'd come to Gayton eight months ago. Abruptly she said, "You'll have to wait." and bustled in, leaving us outside the door. In a few minutes she was back saying, "You'll have to sit in the back in the belfry. There are a few chairs there. Hurry up." We walked through the door just in time. The army was marching up the path. We could hear their boots, then, "Halt" and absolute silence except for Mrs. Browne's peremptory tone giving instructions to the officer in charge. They all filed in and filled the whole church. When we told Uncle Aubrey, he said, "My goodness, I don't think I've ever seen it full, certainly not since Dr. Browne came." Mrs. Browne still paraded up and down the aisles although there was nothing else for her to do. She looked rather like the soldier on the bus. It's a good thing she couldn't hear all the comments as people walked home after the service.

Richard and I near Ulcombe.

Mary and I on her first day going
to school in Northampton.

Mary with her lamb.

(From l. to r.): Uncle Aubrey, Mary, and Auntie Olive.

Our family two years before the war: (from top to bottom) Harold (l.) and Father; Gordon, Mother, Me (l.), and Richard.

Home Farm.

Home Farm House in 1945.

Helen and Mary Semple (on stool) in May 1945.

Mary Chester by the gate leading into the orchard.

The bus we took into Northampton going to school.

Gayton Church where the armies came after their manoeuvres.

My mother soon after the war.

Me, about what I'm like now.

Home Farm
November, 1941

Journal

We aren't having any good news but, because Germany
has invaded Russia, Daddy said, "There's less chance of
Hitler deciding to invade us now." We all knew he might
the summer before last, and for at least a year it was possible. This makes us feel a little better. Everybody here
always listens to the news, especially early in the morning and in the evening.

Now, though, I want to write a little about Mr.
Manning because we all like him so much, but first I'll tell
my earliest memory. The day we moved to Handen Road,
in April, 1934, one of Mummy's best friends, Auntie Tina,
took care of Gordon and Richard and me. Richard was
only six months old, and I wasn't quite two. It was a beautiful day, so we were all out in the garden: Gordon and
David (Auntie Tina's son), Richard in his pram, and me.
Gordon and David decided to play cowboys and Indians,
with them as the cowboys, of course, and me as an Indian.
They quickly captured me and, when they'd tied me to the
dustbin, went off to do whatever they thought cowboys
would do next. It's a big garden. They were way out of
sight and didn't hear my frantic calls. They'd changed
their game and forgotten about their victim. It wasn't un-

67

til what seemed like hours and hours that Auntie Tina heard me crying and came out to rescue me.

Except that Auntie Tina is his daughter and just as kind, that doesn't have much to do with Mr. Manning, so now I'll tell you some things that do. Everybody in England does the washing on Mondays. Mummy says, "That's because Sunday dinner is usually the best one of the week, and there are leftovers for Monday, the day no housewives have time to do much cooking. They just bring out the cold, leftover joint of beef or mutton and fry the leftover vegetables."

Washing at Home Farm starts early, with Uncle Aubrey carrying buckets of water to a farm building that's close to the house. He fills the copper, a boiler, often not made of copper now, that is used to heat water. Then he lights the fire under it. He does this before he goes to oversee the milking of the cows and pasteurize the milk, so he has to be up extra early. By the time he's back for breakfast, Auntie Olive and Mummy have gathered everything that has to be washed, a lot of course, and once everyone has finished breakfast, they go out, warmly dressed at this time of year, and begin the real work of the day. Fortunately Auntie Olive has a washing machine. One of them dips a bucket into the copper and carries it, brimming full, to the washing machine. The other one stuffs in the first load: sheets and pillowcases. Then they take it in turns to tug the handle back and forth, back and forth until they think the load's clean. It has to be taken out and put aside while more water is carried from the copper to top up before putting in the next load. More back and forth with the handle. They usually do three loads in basically the same water. That's because soap powder is hard to come by now. Sometimes they have to grate hard kitchen soap, but that takes a lot of swishing in the water before it dissolves. Once those three loads are done, the water must be siphoned out and rinse water put in. Then there's more turning the handle back and forth. Auntie Olive says, "It's a bit like beating the batter for Yorkshire pudding or cake, only much harder." When that's done, it's all taken out of the washing machine and wrung out by one of them putting it through the mangle. Then it goes into a big wicker basket and has to be carried to the orchard, away up behind the house, and hung on the lines there (always supposing it's not raining). They do this over and over again until everything is washed and hung out.

It's a tremendous job, as Mr. Manning soon realized. So now every Monday morning he goes to the pub a little earlier and comes home carrying two bottles of guinness, "For your elevenses." They sit in the kitchen and just chat until they've drained their bottles, and have enough energy to go back out to the washhouse and finish in time to put a later than usual dinner on the table. Mr. Manning's guinness gives them much more energy than coffee ever did.

Guinness is not the only thing Mr. Manning brings back from the pub. One day he noticed that Auntie Olive and Mummy were giving Richard their bottle tops and asked, "What do you do with them?" Richard said, "Well, I haven't got enough soldiers for two armies, and I'm collecting the bottle tops so they can be an army." "Good idea!" said Mr. Manning, and the next day he came back for dinner carrying Auntie Olive's big shopping basket full to the brim with bottle tops and saying, "I thought you'd need different colours to tell which army was which. There you are. You decide which is us and which is the Germans."

Richard was thrilled and straight after dinner went

into the dining room, where it was very cold because there wasn't enough coal for a fire in there until later in the day. He didn't seem to notice. When I went in to see what he was doing, he was lying on his stomach with a mass of green tops on his right and brown tops on his left. Every now and then he'd move one lot forward and make the other lot retreat. He obviously didn't want to talk to me, so I went back to the warm kitchen to read one of the William books* that Michael Roe had lent me.

Before I began reading though, I was thinking about Mr. Manning being so kind, and I remembered a game we played last Christmas. It's called Coffee Pot. One person goes out of the room, and everybody else decides on a group of homonyms, like two, to, and too, and calls the person back in. He or she asks questions, perhaps, "What's your favourite fruit?" and must be answered, not necessarily truthfully, with a sentence that includes one or more of the homonyms, e.g. "I like pears a lot, but I like plums *too*." Only instead of the homonym they say, "coffee pot."

Well, when it was my turn to guess, I just couldn't and had asked lots of questions without any idea what the words could be. Then I asked Mr. Manning, "When do you think the war will be over?" He answered, "Oh, I don't know. Some people say next summer, but I think that's all my coffee pot and Betty Martin." All the grownups groaned, and someone said, "That does it!" but still I had no idea and had to give up. Mummy said, "It's eye, what you see with, and I, you yourself. Don't you know the say-

*These are books about a very mischievous young boy who was always playing tricks on his family and his friends.

ing, "It's all my eye and Betty Martin?" Mr. Manning thought he was helping me, but I had never heard it. He explained, "It means nonsense—or poppycock." That word was new to me too, but I love it and shall try to find a way to use it next time I'm with Elizabeth or Michael.

Journal

I haven't written anything here for a long time, mostly because I have more homework now. There's lots to write about. This morning at school we were given a big surprise: no homework and the afternoon off, so this evening I have some time. The whole school had a half-holiday because, after weeks of bad weather, the sun was shining at last!

But the news isn't good, certainly not from Africa. The German general, Rommel, is always winning battles, pushing our army further and further back towards Cairo. There are lots of casualties. Daddy thinks we hear too much about the dead and wounded. That it's hard for everyone to know that so many men are losing their lives. He said, "If we had been living in this village during the Crimean War, we would probably only have known about casualties from around here. If two men were in the army and one, say Charlie Munton, was killed in a battle, we'd only know for sure if the other one wrote home, or perhaps we wouldn't even know until a survivor came back. Now every time the wireless is on for the news, we hear about so many losses that it's hard not to grow callous. We can't empathize with so many day after day."

But back to our half-holiday on this glorious day.

Elizabeth and I came home on the 2 P.M. bus, and as soon as we had explained to our mothers why we were early, changed quickly out of our school uniforms and went to a pond where we knew there would be tadpoles. With hair nets tied to broomsticks (this was Mrs. Roe's idea) we scooped up quite a lot to take home, hoping they would turn into frogs. Once we each had some swimming around in big jars, we just went out and sat in the wonderful sun for awhile.

Soon though, Elizabeth said, "Let's walk up to Herbert East's farm. Perhaps the cowslips are out." They were. They are rather like primroses, and I think belong to the same family, but instead of one yellow flower to each stem, several yellowish orange flowers grow up one stalk. The whole field was like a yellow orange sunset. We picked some each, and you wouldn't have known any were gone. We had been to that field together in January because Mr. East always has the earliest lambs. Uncle Aubrey thinks it's too early but, although it was cold and blustery, the new baby lambs were skipping about, suddenly leaping into the air, twisting and turning and almost going head over heels, while their mothers just went on quietly grazing on the cold grass, waiting for their new lambs to come and nuzzle up to them and find a teat. Sometimes there were two or three lambs together, jostling for their milk. Then they'd be back to frolicking.

Now Uncle Aubrey has lambs. Just yesterday evening, Jack George, his shepherd, knocked on the back door, and when Auntie Olive opened it said, looking worried, "Is Arbrey 'ere? I don't know where to pot the ship." Uncle Aubrey wasn't home but should be soon, so Auntie Olive asked the shepherd in, and she and Mummy sat down in the kitchen with him. It was lucky that Uncle Aubrey came soon because they couldn't understand much of what he was saying. Uncle Aubrey and the shepherd left at once, both of them looking anxious. When Uncle Aubrey came back, Auntie Olive asked, "What was that all about? What does 'I don't know where to pot the ship' mean, for goodness sake?" Even though he was obviously very worried, Uncle Aubrey laughed and said, "You're a Northamptonshire woman, and you don't know what he meant! He came to say that he didn't know where to put the sheep. She's about to have her lambs and is in a bad way. He and I'll take turns watching her tonight." When Uncle Aubrey went to take his turn, the ewe was straining hard, so the shepherd stayed, and soon they helped her deliver three lambs. They were perfect, but their mother died.

At breakfast Uncle Aubrey said to Richard and Mary and me, "I want you three to have a lamb each to feed. We'll keep them in the dairy for a day or two." We started right after breakfast when Uncle Aubrey produced three baby bottles and filled them with warm milk saying, "Someone else will do this for you if I'm not around." Then he fetched the lambs and showed us just how to hold the bottles. Fortunately it was Saturday, so we would have two whole days before someone else would have to take over. It was great fun. We'd bring the lambs into the kitchen, and all sit down to hold our bottles the way Uncle Aubrey had shown us. We'd stroke them and make soft sounds to them, loving feeding them as much as they loved being fed.

Actually, nobody needed to feed them while we were at school. We were disappointed when we came home to find that we weren't needed either. Another ewe had had two lambs that didn't live, so the shepherd gave her our three. Sometimes that doesn't work. The ewe refuses to have them, still wanting her own, but soon she was treating them as if they were her own, a good foster mother. Of course we go out to see them in the Home Field and know exactly which ewe will let them have her milk.

Journal

Elizabeth is at boarding school now. I miss her and will only see her during the holidays. Sometimes though, especially when Richard is engrossed with his bottle top armies, Michael and I do things together. The trouble is he can be really bossy. One day in September, after Elizabeth had left, we were on our way back from the slips,[*] where we had gone to see if there were still any blackberries. Before Harold and Gordon went back to Tunbridge Wells, Gordon and I had picked a big shopping basket full, but there were hardly any when I went with Michael. We ate a few and picked a few more for him to take home. He'd brought a little bucket for them. Suddenly, as we were walking up through the bunny field (because there are so many rabbits, that's what Elizabeth named it when she was little) he told me I must carry the bucket, which really annoyed me. They were his blackberries, and the bucket wasn't heavy, so I said, "No, they're *your* berries." He was furious. "I'm older than you," (he's a fortnight older) "and I can tell you what to do. Carry it!" "No. You

*Our name for the railway embankment.

carry it." He threw the bucket down and then pushed me down and sat on top of me.

"You have to do what I say!" Now I was furious and wriggled until I was on top. Then I jumped up and ran home.

The trouble was, I realized as we were having dinner, that there wasn't anybody else to do things with. Uncle Aubrey must have noticed that I was gloomy because he said, "Margaret, we're killing a pig this afternoon. You and Michael might like to watch." As the men who had shares in the pig arrived, I walked up to the Roes' house, knocked on the back door and said to the maid, "Please, will you tell Michael that Uncle Aubrey is killing a pig this afternoon," then turned and ran back down to the farmyard. It wasn't long until Michael arrived, and we stood watching as though nothing had happened in the morning.

It was all a bit gory. The pig made horrible noises when the men brought it from the sty, and louder and louder as three of them held it still. Then one shot it in the neck while another held a bucket to catch the blood. Uncle Aubrey had turned his head away, but we wanted to see everything that was going on. He hated anything to do with butchering, his father's business, and had refused to join him in it. He was only doing it now since he had a share, the biggest one, because he had provided the sty and fed the pig. After they had scalded it with boiling water and scrubbed off all the little hairs, they all helped to cut the pig up, some of it for ham, some for bacon, for chops, ribs, headcheese and trotters. I don't think a morsel was wasted, which made Michael and me remember a rhyme that is going around, now that rationing is stricter and stricter. It starts like a prayer that Dr. Browne sometimes says in church:

77

Dearly beloved brethren, is it not a sin
When we peel potatoes to throw away the skin?
The skin feeds the pigs and the pigs feed us.
Dearly beloved brethren, is it not thus?

Uncle Aubrey even took the bladder, washed it in the horse trough, blew it up and gave it to us for a balloon, a very strong one. By now Richard had abandoned his bottle top armies and he and Mary joined us. We had fun for a week playing with it. The best place to play was in the orchard, tossing it back and forth over the clotheslines (as long as there weren't any clothes on them!) Then, of course, it hit a particularly prickly branch and burst.

Now bacon and hams are curing in the pantry or hanging from the kitchen ceiling. As we were sitting under them at breakfast time on November the 5th, with the wireless on for the 8 o'clock news, it began with the announcement, dramatically given, "Rommel is in full retreat!" Auntie Olive went running up the back stairs, which led right up from the kitchen to Mr. Manning's room, waving the poker, with which she'd been stirring up the fire. She banged on his door and, as soon as she knew he was awake, jubilantly shouted to him the same words as the announcer had used. Then we heard him say, as if that was hard to believe, which it was since our army had always seemed to be the one retreating, "Really? Really?" "Yes, really. Bruce Belfrage just told us." Of course, the minute we'd finished breakfast, Richard made a beeline to his bottle tops to change the ones that were attacking.

Everybody, everywhere we went that day, was excited. Ten days later, to celebrate, the church bells were rung all over Britain, though since then they've stayed silent.

A few days ago Churchill warned, "This is not the end. It is not even the beginning of the end. But it is, perhaps, the end of the beginning."

Journal

My last journal entry told about how excited we all were when Rommel's forces began to be driven back. The first big battle was at El Alamein; in it lots of Italians were taken prisoner. Now some of them are in Prisoner of War camps in England, but many of them are allowed out to help farmers. Uncle Aubrey has two. The closest we can come to their names is Ralph and Ernest. They don't even have to return to the camp each night but stay with Grandma and Grandpa Chester. They're lucky. Grandma Chester is very kind, and she's a wonderful cook. They are paid less than 5 shillings a day, but they can go to the pub sometimes for cigarettes and beer.

Sometimes they come here for a little while, just for a change I suppose, but they hardly know any English (though they are getting better). It's funny if they come when Daddy is here because he thinks if he raises his voice they are more likely to understand. We all like Ernest quite a bit more than Ralph. He has a wife and family and is friendly with Richard and Mary and me. He understood when someone pointed to Mummy and asked, "You have a wife?" He smiled and said, "Yes! Yes!" Then Mummy pointed to us and asked "And children?" He beamed and nodded, holding up two fingers. Ralph comes when Ernest does, but I don't think he wants to. There just isn't much else to do in Gayton. Still, when they had parcels from home, they both gave us a little chocolate and some bread, but that was terribly dry and hard to chew. Ralph seemed most pleased that his parcel had cigarettes in it, and he was obviously glad when nobody here wanted any.

It isn't just El Alamein that has given people here some hope of an end to the war, which we might win now because, near the end of January, the German army in Russia had to surrender. There was a great sense of relief all over the country when that news came. Some cities had parades and speeches, and everywhere there was lots of excitement. Even so we're still being warned that "Careless talk costs lives." There was a cartoon in *Punch*[*] a while ago of two farmers standing near a five-bar gate obviously jabbering away happily, but you could see Hitler's head inside one of the gateposts. With the Russians' victory at Stalingrad, and the Americans fighting in N. Africa now, everybody feels that there is a chance to win. Richard will need more bottle caps. Let's hope there are two more colours, so that it's obvious who the Russians fighting the Germans are, and who the Americans fighting with us are. I'm sure Mr. Manning will get them if it's possible.

There must be an American camp near Northampton because I see lots of American soldiers walking around when I'm on the bus coming home. If we stop at a traffic light near them, they like it if we manage to open the window and say, "Hello." They say, "Hi," and often they offer

[*]This was an English magazine very like the *New Yorker*.

us gum. Some children even go up to them on the street and say, "Got any gum, chum?" Usually they have. We're not allowed to have gum, but sometimes when we say, "No, thank you," they dig into their pockets and pull out a bar of chocolate. That's a real treat because sweets are rationed.

Even though the news is often better now, sometimes it isn't. There is something called a radar screen which is supposed to show where there are German planes flying over to attack, but their pilots have found a way to fly low beneath it. They are bombing more cities north of here now, like Birmingham, but occasionally there are still raids on London. One of their pilots flew in low to bomb a school in Lewisham. Lots of children, and some of the teachers, were killed. Even worse, and something that made everybody here really angry, was when another pilot flew very low and strafed a playground where lots of children and one or two teachers were out for after-lunch playtime. Many of them were killed. Lewisham's so near to Lee that we felt especially bad.

Because of that, nobody in Gayton was sympathetic when, one night early in January, a small German plane, a Messerchmitt (a one-man plane like a Spitfire) crashed just by the side of the lane below the Manor Farm. The firewatchers that night heard a loud crash and went out to see what had happened. They didn't have much trouble finding it because the noise had been so loud they knew where to start searching. When they reached it the pilot was dead, so they came back to the Queen Victoria, where the firewatchers spend the night, and telephoned the fire watching headquarters with the news. In the morning the whole village was agog and mostly glad it had happened.

In the afternoon, when all the other curious people

had been to have a look, Elizabeth and I decided to go and see for ourselves. The plane was easy to find, just past the Bunny Field, where some of the prickly gorse bushes had one or two bright yellow flowers already. What we hadn't expected was that the dead pilot would still be in it. Neither of us had ever seen a dead body. We just looked once, enough to see that he was an ordinary young man in leather clothes, with a leather helmet and a wounded face. To look at him, he could have been from Gayton. We walked almost the whole way back without saying a word, but we did agree that we wouldn't tell anybody what we had seen. We hadn't been specifically told not to go, but we had known that we probably shouldn't.

Journal

Everyone, not just us, is getting really tired of the war. The bombing hasn't been quite as bad, especially for London, but food rationing is more and more severe. We get very little butter, two ounces a week each, and there is a rumour that bread will be rationed soon. Some of the things in short supply, especially cream and butter, are strictly monitored. It's forbidden to make butter. Cream is not to be skimmed off for any reason.

There are "spies," inspectors employed by the government, who go around checking. One went to a farm in Devon, which is famous for its cream as everyone knows, and asked the farmer to sell him some. Because the law is so strict, the farmer said, "No. I can't do that." But the inspector kept on asking. Still "No." Then he said, pitifully, "Please help me. My wife is ill, and her doctors say she must have cream to make her stronger." The farmer, a kind man, gave in, saying, "Well, I suppose I could let you have a quarter of a pint." He was taken to court and fined a lot of money.

Soon after that Auntie Olive had Daddy making butter for us. When Uncle Aubrey brought home a mason jar almost full of cream, which he'd separated at the afternoon's milking, Auntie Olive said, "Now you can make butter, Jamie. We're pretty safe here."

So that evening, when some of us were sitting in the dining room, he had the mason jar and was slowly shaking it from hand to hand like a pendulum. Auntie Olive had warned that it could take a long time, and it did, but that was partly because, just as Daddy said, "I think it's turning into butter at last," we heard a knock at the back door, then voices: Auntie Olive's and the policeman's. We recognized his voice even though he was a bit out of breath.

He'd ridden his bicycle from Blisworth, where he lives, and it's up hill almost all the way.* He was panting, but his voice was loud when he asked, "Is Aubrey in? The Gammages** are making a fuss again. It's probably nothing. You know what they're like, but I'd better hear what Aubrey has to say."

For a moment Daddy looked startled. His almost-butter must not be discovered. He looked around for a hiding place without finding a really good one, so he quickly tucked it behind the curtains, making sure it was out of sight, then whispered to us, "If he comes in, don't let your eyes stray over there." Luckily he didn't come in. As soon as Daddy was sure he had left, he began again, passing the mason jar back and forth, back and forth. Auntie Olive came in to ask if there was butter yet and saw there wasn't. "What, not yet?" So Daddy told her why not.

She said, "Why didn't you sit on it?"

*There weren't any gears on bikes then. It was all done by legs and feet!

**Uncle Aubrey had warned us about them. They didn't want anybody going on their land and might set their dogs on us if we did.

"Sit on it?! First, it would have made it warm, but apart from that, if he'd come in, he'd surely have expected me to stand up and shake hands, not just sit like a broody hen. Anyhow, look: I think it's coming now." Then, triumphantly, "See? It's separating. There's some buttermilk." We had got by with it much better than the poor man in Devon.

There's also a rumour that eggs are in very short supply, that soon the ration may be only one per person every eight weeks. Of course that won't affect us much. Auntie Olive is in charge of the eggs, which means collecting them every day. Often Richard and Mary and I go with her. It's usually fun. The eggs that have only just been laid are warm. We love holding them for a moment or two before they go into Auntie Olive's big basket. In the rick yard there are several hen houses, everyone with a small doorway for the hens, and sometimes the cock, to go in and out. At the back of each house are five or six nesting boxes, where the hens are supposed to lay their eggs. But sometimes one of them turns broody and goes off to find what she thinks will make a good nesting place. Then, after five or six days, she's usually laid six to eight eggs. Auntie Olive doesn't want this to happen too often because a broody hen is not laying an egg for her each day. She's busy keeping those eggs warm. One of our jobs is to watch for broody hens, so that they can be discouraged by having each egg they lay collected by us. Often the hen will go off and find another place. Then we feel really mean when we take those eggs.

Every afternoon when we've finished collecting them, Auntie Olive sits at the kitchen table and wipes each one clean. Then they go into special egg boxes in the pantry until they are collected by a government egg collector. He expects there to be a lot each time. Usually there are because often they aren't collected for about eight weeks. They're edible then, but they can't taste nearly as good as the ones we eat. Of course he pays for the eggs, and Auntie Olive gives us a little pocket money for helping.

One afternoon she couldn't find the key to unlock the nests at the back of one of the hen houses. She looked and looked, but with no luck. "Margaret," she said, "do you think you could manage to wriggle through the hens' front door and push up hard on the flaps above the nests? If I pull maybe we can break them open. Then Aubrey will find another padlock."

I did it, but it was horrible. First of all the hens' door is not meant for an almost eleven year old girl, so I had to wriggle and wriggle; it was such a tight squeeze. Then the floor was disgusting; when I wriggled back out I must have been really stinky, and I felt as if I had all sorts of crawly things all over me. Auntie Olive said, "Ugh, that can't feel good, but well done. You'd better go and have a bath right away, and ask Mummy to put your clothes straight into the wash house. I'm sure she'll help you wash your hair, too. It looks as though you were pulled through a hedge backwards!"

Journal

The Germans are gradually retreating out of Russia. Everybody here is glad about that, but I heard Daddy say to Harold, "Yes, it's certainly good that Russia is on the offensive now, but we have to hope that they don't reach Berlin before we do. Who knows what they might do there."

Harold was here, Gordon and Richard too, for three weeks, because I had scarlet fever, and that's how long we had to be in quarantine, all but the grownups. The boys could be anywhere in the house they wanted to except my bed room, but I had to stay in it the whole time, and not go out for anything! Only Mummy could go in and out, and each time she left she had to wash her hands in a bucket of water she kept just the other side of the damp sheet she had to hang over the outside of the door. Three weeks seemed an awfully long time, but when Elizabeth Roe had it, she was in quarantine for eight weeks! The only possibly good thing for me was that, when we came back from Gayton, Mummy and Daddy and I swapped bedrooms. Theirs is bigger and has two large windows that would have needed yards and yards of blackout material. They decided I could manage without a light on when I went to bed more easily than they could. Luckily I was allowed a torch but had to keep it pointed down. Before I was ill, it didn't take me long to run up from the bathroom and hop into bed. Then I could read under the sheets, but I didn't tell anyone I was doing that. They did begin to wonder why I needed a new battery so often!

While I had scarlet fever the air raids started again. The others would all be downstairs, but Mummy would come up and stay with me. Sometimes we'd play word games like coffee pot, or if it was bedtime she'd read to me until I went to sleep. One of those nights Daddy was on fire-watching duty. When he was helping people out of a house that was on fire in the next road, he looked in this direction and thought our house was on fire. As soon as he possibly could, he ran home. It was only when he turned the corner that he saw there weren't any fires in our road. Our house had looked on fire because the room that faces where he was is the one that I'm in, and it has its thin pre-war curtains, so the flames were reflected off the windows. Mummy told me he was as white as the white of an egg and couldn't stop trembling.

I'd only been at Eltham Hill, my new school, for a fortnight before I had scarlet fever. I don't like the school very much, but maybe that's just because I miss my Northampton friends. I was upset when school started because it was a whole week before Gordon and Richard had to go to Tunbridge Wells (and come back the next week for quarantine). I was even more upset to find I'd been put in the lowest class. This is a school that goes from eleven to eighteen. I had already done everything that class was doing and found it really boring. So Mummy went to see Miss Johnson, the head mistress. She said the first class was right for me because of my age, but somehow Mummy persuaded her that it couldn't be good for me to be bored all the time, and she agreed to let me try the next class.

It's much better, and I really like the English and history teachers. They aren't boring. We're reading some poems in English that I love and, unlike most of the others, I love it when our homework is to learn a poem. One is about a shepherd bringing his flock home for the night. At least that's what it seems to be about, but really it's about sleep, not sheep. I do have a hard time with Latin. The class began it only just before I had scarlet fever, so I missed three weeks. The trouble is Harold and Gordon aren't here to help, and the teacher hasn't offered to. Even so, I'm glad I'm in this class. One problem is that I'm not making any friends, except perhaps the two girls I ride the tram with, Barbara and Myrtle, and I don't think we'll become really close friends. For one thing, they don't much like reading, so we can't talk about books.

Writing about going to school on a tram has reminded me of a story Daddy was told by Mr.White, who comes two or three times a week to do some jobs that Daddy doesn't have time for, like cutting the grass or carrying coal and coke up from the cellar. He used to be a tram driver, and usually he didn't have any problems, but one day he was afraid he was going to be late returning his tram to the depot. A man in a small car, going much slower than Mr.White needed to go, was driving just in front of him, on the rails. So, very frustrated, as soon as they were both stopped at a red light, Mr.White hopped out of his tram, ran up to the little car, knocked for the driver to open the window and said indignantly, "Can't you drive anywhere but on the rails?" There was no apology, just "Yes, mate, and it's more than you can do."

When he was young, Mr.White was an ostler, and even now when he's cleaning shoes, his mouth is slightly open, and he is all the time blowing air out between his teeth. At first we were puzzled about this, until Daddy remembered seeing someone else who had been an ostler doing it and said, "It's habit from when they were brushing the horses. Blowing keeps the horses' hairs from going into the ostlers' mouths. They did it so much they do it now, when they are no longer ostlers, hairs or not."

31 Handen Road
January 29, 1944

Journal

Probably because some of our troops are fighting in the Far East now, we hear quite a lot about the war with Japan. There are suddenly place names we have never heard before. I don't know many, but it seems as though both the U.S. and British forces are taking back places that had fallen to the Japanese. I noticed one place because of its name: Empress Augusta Bay. In English we've just finished reading *The Importance of Being Earnest* by Oscar Wilde. It's very funny. When we read a few scenes aloud I was Aunt Augusta, one of the funniest characters. She behaves as I imagine an empress would. I shall have to look for Empress Augusta Bay in our atlas or on the globe Auntie Cissie and Auntie Jessie gave us for Christmas. They always used to come here for Christmas anyhow, but now they've been bombed out, luckily when there was nobody in the house, so they are living with us.

This was the first Christmas at home since 1938. What a long time! In spite of rationing, Mummy managed to make us a very good Christmas dinner. We had a turkey. They aren't rationed, but we only ever see them at Christmas time. She made Christmas pudding, and Richard found the sixpence hidden in it. At teatime there was

92

even a cake with all the old ornaments on it: Father Christmas with some animals, sheep and lambs and a dog, as if he was a farmer. We hadn't expected there to be stockings at the foot of our beds, but when we woke up, there they were. They mostly had useful things in them like combs and toothbrushes, but there were some sweets: bulls-eyes and acid drops, even some chocolate, which must have been from Daddy and Mummy's rations. But at the bottom there wasn't a tangerine as there always used to be. We hardly ever see grapefruit or oranges or tangerines. They come from the Middle East, and ships in the Mediterranean are in great danger. Now people are beginning to talk about the end of the war, so perhaps it won't be such a long time before ships are safe.

Only here it doesn't seem as though the war is ending. A week or so ago air raids began again. They're being called "the little blitz." So far they are not as bad as the blitz was, but we do often have to get up at night. When the siren wakes us, we all quickly put on dressing gowns and slippers and hurry downstairs. Well, everyone hurries down except Auntie Jessie. She takes ages to dress completely, even putting on her hat and coat and gloves! When the bombs seem closer and there's still no Auntie Jessie, Auntie Cissy goes to the bottom of the stairs and calls out, "Hurry up, Jessie! If we have to leave, it won't be to go to Buckingham Palace." I don't usually mind. In fact if I've been reading in bed, under the covers with my torch, and know there is an exciting part coming but am too sleepy to go on, I'm pleased we are up and I can read some more.

We're glad when it's foggy because that means the German planes can't see their targets and tend to drop their bombs, just to be rid of them and turn home. Of course, that probably means a residential area is hit instead of the docks or buildings in the City, where there are very few people at night. We don't feel good being glad, but we can't help it. Since it means a short raid, I think just about everyone must be glad, but I still worry about being glad to be able to read.*

*Once, at a party, I was talking to a friend of ours, who had lived in London in WWI, when there were Zeppelin raids. I knew she enjoyed reading so I told her, as I had no one else, that I felt, even as I did it, guilty at being pleased at having to be up in the night, even though other people were being bombed out, badly wounded, or killed. She said, "Oh, so did I. So do I."

31 Handen Road
April 29, 1944

Journal

I just met a cousin I didn't think I'd ever seen before. Her name's Margaret too, but she's always called Peggy. One weekend at the beginning of March, Mummy and Daddy went to Tunbridge Wells to see Gordon and Richard and left me at home with Auntie Cissie. I'd finished my homework and been reading a lot but didn't really have anything else I wanted to do. Suddenly, Auntie Cissie said, "I know; I'll ring Peggy and ask if we can go to see her." She vanished into the study and closed the door after her, so I couldn't hear what she was saying and went back to my book. In about five minutes she came out smiling and said, "Yes, she'd love to have us, for tea." We decided that it had better be fairly early, so that we could be back before there might be an air raid. "You go and spruce up a little while I find some biscuits." Nearly every one going unexpectedly to a meal nowadays takes something with them.

Peggy lives in Croydon which is where Auntie Cissy's school is. That meant we only had to go to the end of the road to catch the bus. We were lucky. A bus soon came, and it was able to go all the way on the normal route. If there's bomb damage on the route, the buses are diverted. That happened not long ago at Lee Station when the railway bridge was bombed and hanging down into the road. Only for a day though. Miraculously it was repaired overnight, and by the next morning the trains could run over it, and the buses could run under it. It's quite a long way to Croydon and buses stop frequently. Auntie Cissie goes on that route to school every day, an hour each way, and she told me we would see a lot of air raid damage, but also that there would be pretty front gardens with daffodils and tulips and even some with wallflowers, which I love. The Roes had all the beds in their front garden full of them, yellow, orange and dark red ones, every spring. They were like beautiful counterpanes.

The journey didn't take as long as it does when Auntie Cissy goes in the week because there weren't as many people getting on and off the bus. We arrived sooner than we had expected, and when Bobby, who's seven, opened their front door, he called out to his mother before he let us in, "They're here already," and Peggy came running from the kitchen in her apron and drying her hands. "Oh, good. You must have made record breaking time. Come in. Come in." And, as soon as she'd kissed Auntie Cissie, she gave me a big hug saying, "Margaret, how you've grown! Well, of course you have. You were only four the last time I saw you. Let's go into the lounge. Bobby, please show them in there and then put their coats on our bed, while I put these biscuits away. They're a wonderful gift, but you shouldn't have bothered. If you don't mind, I think I'll keep them until Eric is back. We have plenty for tea, and he gets so little homemade food. He's on leave and went to see a friend of his, but I think he'll be home before you have to go." As we followed Bobby to the lounge, we saw that the dining room table was already laid, and it certainly looked as though there was plenty of food. I saw bread and butter and jam and a cake

96

that looked homemade. Bobby is shy and was obviously relieved when his mother arrived. He hardly said anything until after tea, but then he showed me his trains and even let me wind up the engines for him before he set them on different rails, and he told me, "Daddy gave me these when he came home on leave." Then, very proudly, "He's in the navy." Soon after that he shouted, "Daddy, Daddy," and running to the door to greet him, jumped up into his arms for a kiss. Eric is an officer and looked very smart in his uniform.

We only stayed a little longer, until Auntie Cissy said, "We'd better be off. We ought to be home before it's really dark." On the bus she explained why we'd left so soon after Eric came home. "His leave is almost over, so I thought they should just be their family. It must be hard for them all: for him to leave when he knows that there are air raids still, and for Peggy and Bobby not to know when they'll see him again. Peggy knows it may be if they see him again. She must be doubly anxious because her father, our father's elder brother, Harold, died as a result of mustard gas soon after the end of the Great War." She paused and then said, "I do hope we didn't eat too much of their rations."

*　　*　　*

That all happened before the Easter holidays. By then, thank goodness, the "Little Blitz" was almost over. We haven't heard the sirens for nearly a fortnight. Perhaps the Luftwaffe has other things to do. The Germans have occupied Hungary to try to stave off the Russians' advance, but they still have another army retreating from Russia, and of course they occupied most of the rest of Europe long ago. Richard must be spending a lot of time

97

lying on the floor to change the positions of his bottle tops. I'm surprised at how much I miss him. Luckily before he went to school in Tumbridge Wells, Harold and Gordon had moved to a much better billet. They had been very unhappy in their first one and not very happy in the second one. The third one, with an elderly couple and their daughter, Mrs. Bennett and her daughter Shirley, was much better.

There was one very good part of the holidays. Mrs. Bennett sort of swapped Gordon and Richard for me, and I had a wonderful week with Shirley. Except for when we were asleep, I don't think we stopped talking. Well, perhaps at meal times. Shirley and her mother live with Shirley's grandparents, so there are three grown ups, and of course we didn't talk if they were talking. We went to the swimming bath a few times and went down the chute over and over again, which was great fun. But I think we both thought the best thing we did in the whole week was sleeping out one night in a small tent in the garden. For a while we lay with our heads outside the tent flaps and gazed at lots and lots of stars, wondering if they all had names, before we wriggled back in and climbed under the blankets. After we'd jabbered until we couldn't stay awake any longer, we seemed to just stop at the same moment. We were talking about *The Wind in the Willows,* which we both love and had each read a couple of times. Shirley's favourite character is Rat. Mine is Mole; he's so happy-go-lucky, doing things on the spur of the moment, like suddenly stopping spring cleaning because it was a beautiful day, and setting out for the Wild Wood on a grey winter day because the other animals talked about it, but he'd never been there. In the morning we both woke up early and continued where we'd left off: about what happened when he did that. We just never seemed to run out of things to talk about.

Now that I'm home and Gordon and Richard are back in Tunbridge Wells, I really am glad to be back at school, in spite of not liking it much.

Journal

This has been a strange week. We were jubilant about D-Day. Our armies are in France at last and on their way to Paris, then Berlin. Only now: more horror. When I came home from school a few days ago, the dining room table was gone and something that looked like a table, but bigger, had taken its place. The top was made of brown steel and the back and sides of a strong metal mesh, with the front mostly open for crawling in and out. Mummy had already found a mattress that fitted and put it inside.

As soon as he was home from the city, Daddy said, "It's called a Morrison Shelter. It should save us from anything but a direct hit. I think it's better than the Anderson Shelters people have had since the blitz. They're out of doors, so pretty cold in the winter, and if it rains, they're often flooded. There are rumours that the Germans have a new kind of plane. It's supposed not to have a pilot. When it's over its target, its engines suddenly stop, making the plane plunge to earth and destroy everything where it lands. With this new shelter, we ought to be safe unless one lands on our roof, though there may be a lot of debris. When I ordered it I hoped we'd never have to use it, that they were only rumours we were hearing about Hitler's new weapon. We all hoped he was bluffing just to scare us. After all, he'd said he'd be living in Buckingham Palace by August 15th, 1940."

Because the siren went off, for two or three nights we got up and went down stairs, to sit for an hour or two in the lounge, some of us reading and some nodding off into a kind of sleep. Then all of a sudden, on Friday night, Daddy exclaimed "Quick, we must go into the shelter," and hustled us all into the dining room. It was the half-term holiday; Gordon and Richard were home, and so was Harold because he's at Cambridge now, and his term has ended. Then, Auntie Jessie and Auntie Cissie have both been living with us since they were bombed out, and Grandma had come because Mummy was worried about her being alone. That made nine of us. The shelter was meant for four!

Of course it took us a while to scramble in and try to make room for everybody. By the time we were all scrunched in together, the sound Daddy had heard was diminishing. We could breathe again and try to sort ourselves out. We all, even Grandma, had our knees under our chins, but Daddy thought we had better stay in the shelter until the all-clear sounded.

He was right. Soon after the first plane had gone over, we heard another coming, but all of a sudden we couldn't hear anything until there was an enormous crash which sounded horribly close. That was followed by several more planes seeming to cut their engines right above us. We learned to count the time from the silence to the huge explosion: five seconds, through which we all held our breath, then simultaneously breathed sighs of relief. But we knew there must be people, not far away, who *hadn't* miraculously escaped. The Germans call these ghastly things V1s. It seems there's to be another kind soon.

101

Well, if there was anything lucky about this, it was that we were all able to make up a little for the long scary night. It was Saturday, so no one had to go to work or school. Still, I'm pretty tired; I think I'll stop now.

A Few Days Later

Here I am, back again, but still tired. The V1s keep coming. On Monday when I went to school, we were met at the door by our gym teacher who held up her hand to stop us going in. "Good morning girls. I'm so glad to see you all today. Wait just a moment until there are a few more of you." We stood waiting, with no idea why, until a dozen or so of us were gathered there. "Now, girls, I have to tell you of a change. Go in as quietly as possible and straight along the corridor to the stairs, then up to the first floor. All our classes will be up there for a while. All right, in you go. Remember, quietly now."

Inside we found that the whole ground floor had been taken over for an emergency hospital. The corridor reeked of disinfectant and nurses were scurrying from room to room. Through the doorways we could see beds and stretchers, and one side of the corridor was lined with gurneys and casualties, who were mostly facing the wall. One woman, who didn't have her face to the wall, looked grey and very tired. It's been like this every day this week, except that the people are always different. We walk past as quietly as we can, trying not to stare. Many of the people are sent to real hospitals where they can get more care than here, but every morning all the beds and gurneys are full again, and all our classes are upstairs now.[*]

---

[*]At the time, I didn't realize that doing this day after day had been anything but a routine. Then many years later, Dick and I went to a movie, *Operation Crossbow,* a treat for us in the early '60s. We knew nothing about it, except that some friends recommended it. The movie, it turned out, was about this stage of the war. Soon after it began, there was a scene that could have been filmed at my school in 1944. We were sitting quietly watching when suddenly I broke into great, heaving sobs that I couldn't control. Dick grabbed my hand and quietly led me out of the cinema.

Journal

There haven't been so many of us since the second night of flying bombs. Gordon and Richard went back to Tumbridge Wells, but almost at once they were reevacuated to Frome in Somerset. Auntie Jessie is back in Enfield. That's north of London, and it's pretty safe. It's the places south of London that are in trouble when engines cut out sooner than they were supposed to. Grandma has decided she'd rather be home in her own bed even if there's no protection there. I don't blame her; sometimes I feel as if I'd rather be in mine.

There are only five of us now, and Mummy thought that, rather than us all be uncomfortable for the whole of every night, we should take it in turns to sleep in the shelter. Actually, I don't have to take turns because the others think that as I'm still growing I should have as much sleep as possible. It's supposed to work like this: Auntie Cissie and Daddy and I (because we go off to work or school each morning) share the first shift. Mummy and Harold are in the lounge on camp beds and are supposed to come in with us when they hear the warning or hear a doodlebug (everyone is calling them that now), coming without any warning. Well, this plan doesn't really work. I don't go off to sleep very soon because Auntie Cissie and

Daddy do, and they both snore loudly but not together and not with the same kind of snore, which would be far better than the duet they perform. Daddy goes onk, onk, onk, or something like that, and Auntie Cissy replies in a sort of rising, trembly noise, like someone starting to sing a scale but getting stuck on the third note and ending with a snort; so on and on and back and forth. It would be funny if it didn't make it so hard to go to sleep. I wish I could make a recording to play back to them once the war is over, as it surely will be soon now that our army and the American army are in France.

The plan has also failed because the people on the camp beds are far more comfortable and sleeping far more soundly, for they don't hear either the siren or a stray doodle-bug. This means that someone from the shelter must crawl out of it and go to wake them up. Of course that will make five people, so nobody lies down then. We're also a little more cramped for space because Daddy, who has just bought Harold an expensive French dictionary in two large volumes, insists on having it in the shelter where it takes up about as much room as I do when I'm sitting up. This would be funny, too, if it weren't so uncomfortable.

Still, it's much better than the first night was. Auntie Cissie and Daddy seem to manage to go off to work without feeling too terrible, and Mummy copes with shopping and eking out the rations to make us good meals, as well as many other chores. It helps that Auntie Cissie has dinner at school, and Daddy has his in the city. They both say it's not very good, but it means we can all have a better supper. Harold studies quite a lot; that's what the long summer vacation is supposed to be for. There are some daytime raids, but it's not as bad as at night. I can still go to school and come home for lunch much the way I have all this year.

The doodlebugs are aiming for central London, but often they don't reach there. That's when they plunge to the ground near us. Often many come in over Croydon, where Auntie Cissie's school is, and sometimes they crash to the ground there. Gordon and Richard's school in Tumbridge Wells was in a pathway too. That's why they have been re-evacuated to Frome in Somerset. They like the people where they are billeted very much. Since he and Harold weren't at all happy in their first two billets, I'm sure Gordon must be relieved.

Journal

Mummy and Daddy decided that, if Auntie Olive and Uncle Aubrey agreed, I should go back to Home Farm. Mummy said, "We don't think it's safe enough for you here while there are so many air raids. There seem to be as many buzz-bombs (another name for them) during the day now as at night. We don't like you going off to school alone." I didn't much like it either, and I don't much like them still being in London, but Gayton *is* my most favourite place. As soon as Mummy can arrange it, I am to go back to Northampton High School. I like it much better there than Eltham Hill, and there are never any air raids on Northampton. There isn't much reason to bomb it. Mostly they make only shoes and beer, lots of beer! There are two big breweries. There's always a yeasty smell in the air, and on Bridge Street every other doorway is a pub! The Germans have discovered how to carry the buzz-bombs part of the way on other planes and then release them to attack cities further north than London, but not Northampton. It's supposed to be one of the safest towns in England.

In 1941, when Coventry was almost demolished and its magnificent cathedral completely destroyed, everyone was afraid for other cities and towns. Uncle Aubrey could see we were scared. He said, "I don't think we have to worry about Northampton. It is low compared with most towns. There's supposed to be a covering of mist, so that from the air it looks like a lake." It's good to know that now. We had wondered if pilots might smell the beer, but the doodle bugs certainly won't!

I'd better stop here instead of running on and on. Tomorrow I'm going in to stay with Auntie Katie for a day or two. She invited me when she realized that all my Gayton friends would be in school.[*]

---

[*]For my grandchildren: You'll be amazed that in England the spring term doesn't end until the third week of July! But we didn't have to go back to school until the third week of September. Except that when I went to Eltham Hill I had to go a week before the boys went back.

Journal

Even though the allies have been in France since D-Day, they seem to us to be advancing very slowly. The V1s and now, since September, even worse flying bombs, V2s, are devastating London and some cities north of here. Auntie Cissy's school has been evacuated again because sometimes doodlebugs fall in Croydon, though they are meant for central London. The allies finally took the Pas-de-Calais, where the V1s were launched, but there's another launching site in Holland, and the Germans are furiously defending that. There are lots and lots of casualties in London. After Mummy and Daddy have been here for the weekend and return to London, I'm horribly aware of the danger they are in. When they reach Euston, Daddy goes straight to his office, and Mummy goes home, worried whether there still is any home. Once I heard her say to Auntie Olive, "When I'm walking home from the station, I wonder all the way whether our house will still be there."

Because some flying bombs are crashing in or near Tunbridge Wells, Mrs. Bennett wrote to Mummy asking if she could possibly find somewhere in Gayton for Shirley to stay for the summer holidays. There's absolutely no room at Home Farm with all of us here. Thank goodness

Mummy and Daddy are here now for a kind of summer holiday, so we are packed in like too many baby birds in one nest. Mummy and Auntie Olive talked over the possibilities, not many, but at last Auntie Olive said, "Oh, perhaps the Thomases will have her. Avis must be about Margaret and Shirley's age." Mummy went straight off to talk to Mrs. Thomas. I liked this idea because the few times I've been to their house I've liked her. They live just out of the village, a little way past the church, so it's only a short walk. Mrs. Thomas agreed at once, and Mummy went to Grandma and Grandpa Chester's house to use their phone; there are only about three in the village, and the one public phone is unreliable. Shirley arrived the next evening with Daddy and, after she'd had something to eat with Richard and Mary and me, Mummy and I took her to the Thomases.' Now she was an evacuee! Unfortunately Shirley and Avis didn't like each other very much, but Mrs. Thomas and Avis didn't seem to mind that Shirley spent most of her time with us. I think Mrs.Thomas realized that Shirley knew us and felt more at home with us, and Avis was pleased not to have to share her brother and sister. They go to boarding school and are only home in the holidays.

Just before the holidays were over, Harold and Gordon thought it would be fun for us all to go for a bike ride. Even the fact that none of us has a bicycle stopped them. It was to happen on the next day, which the weather forecast said should be sunny. The Roes had other plans and immediately offered to lend us their bicycles, four or them! Then it turned out that, although her elder brother and sister were eager to come, Avis wasn't, so Shirley could have her bike. Voila! It was all arranged. On the chosen day, the weather cooperated, and straight after lunch, we rode down to the Thomases and collected

Shirley, Veronica and Trevor. Harold had been pouring over some road maps of Uncle Aubrey's, and he and Gordon decided that we should go to see the village where Grandma Howlett Jones had grown up. It turned out to be much further away than it looked on the map. Except when we were going down hills, we pedaled and pedaled and pedaled. By no means was everything downhill. (Just as well, really, because we had to come back). After we had arrived in our grandmother's village and seen the manor house where Harold and Gordon thought she had worked for a while, we turned back but hadn't gone very far when Harold decided to look at the map, yet again, to see if there was a shorter way to Gayton. "Yes! I think so, as long as we take a shortcut across a field that's just down this road." Of course, his "just down this road" was about a mile. When we found the field, all the bicycles had to be lifted over a style. Then we cycled in a long line on the bumpy footpath to another style. On and on we went with Harold not being sure where we were, and probably his leg was hurting and he was as tired as we were. We still had double summer time, but even so it was beginning to get dark. We were all starving. Trevor and Veronica, who had always lived around here, didn't recognize anything, and of course the rest of us didn't. Everybody was relieved when we came to Blizworth. When we had slogged up the hill and finally rode into the Thomases' driveway, it was really dark.

Mr. Thomas wrenched open the front door. He was furious with Harold. "What do you mean by keeping Veronica out so late? You promised to be back for supper. What have you been doing?" All Harold could say was, "I'm sorry. We got lost." To which Mr. Thomas replied, "Get lost now!" and herded Veronica, Trevor and Shirley into the house. At Home Farm they were only worried

111

that we'd be really tired and hungry and pleased that Harold hadn't been too much bothered by his leg.

Mentioning Harold's leg reminds me of something else. For a long time now the munitions factories have needed more metal than Britain can come up with, and every household is asked to give old saucepans and anything else metal that they can spare. All the London squares, where before only the residents with keys could go into the central gardens, have been wide open for two or three years. People weren't asked but had to give up any metal railings and gates. That meant our front gate, and the Home Farm front gate, and the Roes' front gate, as well as others in the village. So, when some people moved into a house last year, which they had had built between Home Farm orchard and the Roes' field, and had metal railings and a metal gate installed, nobody in the village felt very friendly towards them. They have a son, Donny, who's about seventeen, and he hasn't made any friends yet. Everyone is guessing about what his father must do. What makes it possible to have all this visible metal? They are being called the Aluminiums because nobody seems to know their name yet.

Well, one Friday afternoon in September, Donny came to the front door with an invitation for Mummy and Daddy and me to go to tea on Saturday. He said half past four would be about right. We're not sure how they knew Mummy and Daddy would be here, but they did. Daddy wasn't keen to go because Uncle Aubrey was harvesting and Daddy loves to help. He stands in the wagon with two or three of the men, and they pack the forkfuls of wheat or barley as they are handed up. The packers have to arrange them smoothly, being careful not to tread on the grain, while they rise higher and higher until those on the ground can't reach to give them any more. Then the ostler walks the horse and its load back to the rick yard where there are other men building ricks. Daddy would much rather have been doing this than going out to tea. He resented that even more, much more, when we found out why we had been invited.

There was some small talk, and then Mrs. Aluminium wheeled in a trolley. As soon as it was cleared away and she returned, Mr. Aluminium asked, "How old is Harold?" Mummy said, "Eighteen." "I thought so," said Mr. A., and then turned to Daddy, "How did you keep him from being called up?" I've never seen Daddy's face look the way it did then, really stony, like an unnamed gravestone, when he replied, "I would never do that. Harold was deferred because he is crippled. I don't know how you can have failed to notice. It's obvious that he has to favour one leg." "Oh," was all that Mr. A. could say, looking very disappointed. How was he to have Donny deferred? Almost at once we stood up, thanked them for tea and left, "shaking the dust from off our feet."

Daddy and many other people think this is a holy war, especially since we're hearing more and more about German atrocities, Japanese ones too. The BBC doesn't tell us much, but there are awful stories in the papers. Sometimes I read them though I don't really want to, but I can't stop myself. We hardly ever talk about it.That's not a very good place to end, but now I'm going to walk to Blizworth Station with Mummy and Daddy. I hate saying goodbye when I know what they are going back to. I walk back up the hill to Gayton with a horrible sinking feeling.

Home Farm, Gayton
January 14, 1945

Journal

We have just started back to school after lovely long Christmas holidays. Mummy and Daddy and all the boys came and it was wonderful all being together. There were parties again, and we had one at Home Farm, though we didn't need quite as much cheering up as we did when I wrote about the parties we had earlier in the war. Surely it's going to end soon. Now though, I want to write about Kirtons' bus.

Before we returned to London in 1943, I only went back and forth to school on a United Counties bus. It comes out to Gayton from the big bus station three times a day. It was that 8 A.M. bus that Elizabeth and I were on during the manoeuvres.

There is another bus that is run by a man named Phil Kirton and his sister, which is called simply Kirtons' bus. It goes into Northampton very early, taking all the people working in factories, who must be on the job even before the United Counties bus has left to come out to Gayton. Kirtons' bus starts in their home village, four or five miles from Gayton and returns in the evening, often with at least one more passenger: me. It leaves Northampton at about the same time as the U.C. bus, but its first stop is

114

Gayton, so it gets there quite a bit sooner. Riding on Kirtons' bus is a wonderful experience, except that when I go on it, I have to stay at school until half past five. There's only one supervised room, which is where people with detentions must go, so I go there, too. Luckily, I've never had a detention (yet), and I can always get a lot of homework done. Usually the teacher on duty isn't very pleased I'm there. The others all leave before I do, which means she has to stay for extra time. It's always obvious that she's anxious for me to go! One of them, usually says, "Margaret, can't you go now? Surely you can wait ten minutes more at the bus stop!"

Kirtons' bus stops outside the Plough Hotel and hardly ever arrives there more than two minutes before it should leave. So I say, "I'm sorry, but Mummy told me that I shouldn't be hanging around there for long, especially when it's dark." Well, sometimes I arrive there a minute or two before the bus does, but often it's there already. I can see it from the top of the hill and run as fast as I can, hoping against hope that some one will see me and ask Mr. Kirton to wait. It would be awful if he left without me because there isn't another bus until morning. Fortunately for me there is a woman whose factory closes after the others, and she's just about always late. To save time (everyone is anxious to be home), two or three men open the emergency exit at the back of the bus, climb down and encourage her: "That's it Dolly," as she, quite a bit overweight, hurtles down the hill, "Keep it up, You're nearly here, my duck." The second she arrives they boost her aboard, often accompanied by cheers, and her rescuers scramble up after her. Usually, by now, all the seats are filled. In fact there are mostly three or four people to each two seats, and the aisle is chock full of people standing. This makes it a major task for Miss Kirton to collect return tickets and issue single ones, like mine, and I'm generally at the back of the bus. But Miss Kirton is very small and manages to wriggle amongst those who are standing, smile frequently and never have a single hair displaced. I always go to the back of the bus because there are two kind men there, and one or other always offers to have me on his lap (as long as there's no one else ensconced). One I knew already. He was Uncle Aubrey's shepherd, so working all day in a munitions factory is a big change for him. If he sees me standing, he says, "Cum on, my duck, plenty o' room 'ere."

Kirtons' bus has been running for at least forty years. When you look at it, coming or going, its sides bulge out as though two immensely fat passengers are sitting on each seat, and no wonder: while so many people were traveling on it to work, it must have been carrying many, many more people than was intended. It's also badly in need of a paint job. Once upon a time it must have been a nice bright scarlet. Now it's a sort of murky plum colour.

Almost always I enjoy riding on this bus, but just occasionally I'm worried all the way to Gayton. In the winter, if there isn't a moon, it's pitch black outside. The headlights, masked in tissue paper and only pointing down, are no help, and no light shines from anywhere else. Most often I know where to get off. I'm the only one who gets off there but know when to start wriggling from the back to the front of the bus, past all those standing in the aisle. The other man who often provides me with a lap if he's there, gets off about two minutes before I do. The trouble is he's not always there, so I have to try to tell when we make a ninety-degree turn at the church. I do always manage this, but it's a great relief when I'm safely down on the road only a little way from Home Farm and,

116

once I'm in the door, see what seem like really bright lights.

I think anyone would agree that Kirtons' bus is unique. One Saturday, while she was still living at Home Farm, Mummy went into Northampton for the day to run some errands. On Saturdays, Mr. Kirton provides extra bus service, leaving Gayton mid-morning and returning around five o'clock. There are fewer passengers than on weekdays, so there's a seat for everyone. The bus was about halfway there when it ground to a totally unscheduled stop. Out went Mr. Kirton to discover what was wrong. Everybody sat patiently while he spent a long time with his head under the bonnet. Eventually he got back on the bus and announced, "Well, I think I've found the problem. We can carry on if someone has some string." There was a long silence while men searched their pockets, and women their handbags. Then suddenly Mummy realized she had with her a parcel to be posted in Northampton. Proudly, she said, "I have some," and proceeded to untie the parcel and present the string to Mr. Kirton. He disappeared under the bonnet again for a few minutes, then climbed back on the bus, started it, accompanied by loud cheers from all the passengers, and they continued on their way.

I'm rattling on, but never mind, it's a "When icicles hang by the wall" day, so we're indoors. My English class has just read that poem. It's by Shakespeare and describes the bitterly cold weather we're having. Winter in Stratford on Avon (not very far away) must have been much like winter in Gayton.

Before I stop, I must write of the absolutely best thing about Kirtons' bus. For a week or two before Christmas, once the bus was well on its way home, there would be Christmas caroling, though not the kind we usually hear. Suddenly some one at the front of the bus would start "Hark the herald angels sing," and before they finished the first verse, the back of the bus would chime in, but with a different carol, often "Good King Wenceslas," and sing all ten verses. The front of the bus had finished their carol before we were well underway! So they started again with, maybe "Away in a Manger," while we were only on our fifth or sixth verse. As soon as we came triumphantly to "Shall yourselves find blessing," we only paused to catch our breath before beginning, perhaps "We Three Kings," with each group singing louder and louder. This "harmony" continued every evening, but I was only there for about its first week, until the school Christmas holidays began. It was a wonderful way to lead up to Christmas!

I have to stop, but I'm sure, if I really thought about it, there'd be more Kirtons' bus stories.

Journal

Everyone here thought the war would be over by now. After all, Paris was freed last August, but it all seems to be happening at a snail's pace. There are different allied armies throughout western Europe. Even so the Germans are retreating very slowly. We're cheered up a bit because a U.S. army has crossed the Rhine into Germany and is on the way to Berlin, and the Russians are advancing rapidly from the North East. There's lots for Richard to do with his armies now, but I don't see him do it now that he's in Frome. I miss him. I miss the whole family, in spite of Home Farm being such a good place to be.

January and February were very cold; overnight even the kitchen windows frosted over. Auntie Olive showed Mary and me how to heat farthings and halfpennies and press them against the windows to make tiny peepholes. The whole world outside was covered with frost that, until it had evaporated, sparkled in the sunlight. One morning when Uncle Aubrey came home from milking, he brought a kingfisher he'd found frozen to death. It was beautiful, with green and red feathers and a spiky beak. What a shame it had died. March is being much better. Spring has arrived, but there are still V2s. I know the boys are safe, but I know Mummy and Daddy aren't, and that's always in the back of my mind.

Still, I've made some wonderful new friends. This is how it happened. At school after the Lower Third, there are two of each class. For the couple of weeks before the summer holidays that I was back at Northampton High School, I was with my friends in the Lower Fourth, but when we went back to school in September, I was in the other Upper Fourth and didn't really know anyone. On the first day Miss Blake announced that we could choose the person we'd like to sit with. (The desks are double, so for two girls). If someone had been chosen by more than one person, Miss Blake would decide who was to sit with her. Everyone except for me wrote her choice on a slip of paper and handed it in. I didn't because I didn't know anyone.

The next morning, Miss Blake read the result and then announced, "Margaret, no one wants to sit with you." I don't know what my face looked like, but I felt awful, until very quickly, someone said, "I'd like to sit with her," and so it was settled, and that's how I met two of my best friends, Helen Semple and her sister Mary, who's in the Lower Fourth.

What's especially good is that they live in Blisworth, about half a mile up the road on the other side from Gayton of the main road, so we're on the same bus each morning. You'd think we'd have known each other before this year, but by the time they're on the bus, it's cram-jammed, and we just never were close together. We didn't even walk the same way from the bus station because Mary Chester started coming with me in September. She goes to the building for the youngest classes, which is on another street, so I deliver her there before going to our building.

Since Elizabeth Roe is only home in the holidays, if Mummy and Daddy aren't here for the weekend, I often

120

go to the Semples' on Saturdays and am sometimes invited for the night. Mr. and Mrs. Semple are Scottish, and I like the way it sounds, but at first it was hard to understand what they were saying. Helen and Mary were born in England and only have slightly Scottish accents. Their farm isn't as big as Uncle Aubrey's, but he has two really: Home Farm and the Manor Farm. Mr. Semple doesn't have many farm workers, but Helen can drive the tractor already, and last autumn when they were finishing the harvesting, she often worked on Saturdays. She's more than a year older than me, and lots of farm children drive by the time they're thirteen or fourteen, especially now that some of the farm hands have been called up.

There are quite a lot of things that are different from Home Farm. Because they are so far out of the village, they don't have electric lines. They do have a generator, but it only provides light for the kitchen and the building where they milk the cows. They have glass lamps in the lounge and the dining room but use candles upstairs. One of Helen and Mary's jobs is to clean and refill the lamps. "We do it every day in the winter but not much in the summer," Mary told me. I've helped them a few times, but it makes me nervous because we carry all the lamps into the dining room and put them on newspapers on the table, where they have to be carefully cleaned and filled with oil.

It's lovely being there now that the days are beginning to be longer; the lamps don't need quite so much attention, and we are outside a lot. We often go for walks, some on the farm and sometimes a little way up the road to Blisworth Woods, but after Ulcombe's many woods with huge trees, they don't seem like much more than a copse. There aren't any woods here like the ones in Ulcombe where we went with Auntie Grace to find chest-

121

nuts or to pick primroses. I like walking round the fields with Helen and Mary, especially now that the crops are beginning to grow and there are lots of green shoots. Their bull is sometimes out in a field all by himself. Mary said, "We never walk in this field when he's here." He's enormous and fearsome. Once I saw him led across the farmyard, pulling hard on the rein, stamping his feet and tossing his head a lot. It made me glad Uncle Aubrey doesn't own a bull but pays for one to come from another farm.

I should stop now but wanted to write about the school play. We did *Richard the Second* and, although most of the parts were played by girls in the fifth and sixth forms, Mary and I were in it. Mary was a page and helped hold a canopy over the new king, Henry IV, but, since she didn't have a speaking part, she didn't have to go to many rehearsals. I was Henry Percy, which is only a small part, even smaller with a lot cut from the play, but I did have to be at rehearsals quite often because I said a few words in three or four scenes. In the play Bolingbroke returns from exile to fight King Richard for the crown, so a lot of it is about war. It made me think how different war was then from now. Many men were killed on both sides, but wars were fought on foot or on horse back. Women weren't in the armies and there weren't any aeroplanes with bombs or any long range weapons. All very different.

Now I must stop rambling on. Mummy and Daddy are coming for the weekend, and if I go now, I can meet them on their way up from Blizworth station. Even when it's dark, I like to do this because then we have a little while when it's just the three of us. Oh, I do hope the war will be over soon and we'll all be back at home.

Journal

Hurrah for V-E Day. At school on May 7th, we were told that if the news came that morning, we'd have the rest of the day off (everybody knew that the war in Europe was over, but the documents weren't signed yet) so we were all hoping it would happen that night because then we'd have the whole next day off. It was like it is on Christmas Eve when you go to bed desperately hoping that you'll be given the present you want more than anything else in the world. When I went to bed it still hadn't happened, but I told Auntie Olive that if the war officially ended before school the next day, I wanted to go home. She knew I'd stay awake and left the wireless on loud so that I could hear the news. At nine o'clock there it was. I heard her running up the stairs the way she had to tell Mr. Manning, "Rommel is in full retreat!" She burst in as I jumped out of bed. We danced round the bedroom and hugged and hugged each other and then planned for the morning. I'd have to be up really early and ring Mummy and Daddy to say I wanted to come. That wouldn't be easy. There are only about three telephones in the whole village and an unreliable public phone. There were only two I thought I could ask to use so early in the morning. Uncle Aubrey woke me up before he left for milking. That had to go on even if the whole rest of the country had a holiday. I went to the Roes' house, the nearest, first, even before Mrs. Roe wasn't up, but she didn't mind at all and gave me a big hug and waltzed me around the kitchen, but when I tried to phone nothing happened. Their phone was dead. So, from there I ran further up the road and round the corner to Grandma and Grandpa Chester's house. They *were* up. More hugs, and then I tried their phone. It worked but the lines were all tied up. Now I was really worried. Unless I'd talked to Mummy or Daddy, I couldn't go. I was going to have to get across London from one side to the other and couldn't possibly do that all by myself, at least not with the huge crowds that were expected. Grandma Chester gave me a cup of tea and sat down with me until at last, after two or three useless tries, I got through. Daddy said, "Of course. I'll meet you at Euston, right where you have to hand in your ticket."

I thanked Grandma Chester, kissed her and rushed back to Home Farm, where Auntie Olive had breakfast waiting for me. Mary was still asleep and didn't know yet that there'd be no school. I choked down a little food, ran upstairs for my toothbrush, and ran as fast as I could, a mile and a half to the station. As I puffed out what I needed at the ticket window, I could hear the train coming, grabbed my ticket, flew up the steps and across to the crowded platform on the other side of the lines, just in time. The train was pulling up. It looked full already, but somehow everybody waiting was crammed in, most of us only as far as the corridor, but we were on the train!

It hadn't gone far before a woman near me noticed how pale I was. I was feeling horrible and apparently had turned an ominous shade of green. Opening the door of the carriage right by us a little, she called out, "Can you manage to fit in another sardine? This child looks as if she'll faint." That must have been how I felt, though I never had fainted, so it hadn't occurred to me. She grabbed my arm and somehow squeezed me through the door. Luckily one of the men in air force uniform pulled me a little way further and saying, "Come on then, Luv, sit on my knees," hoisted me there. After a few minutes I didn't feel so strange, but when I said, "I can stand now, thank you," he said, "No need. Just stay here until we reach Euston." A little bit later, one of the men, there were only men, all in uniforms, some army, some air force, started singing, and gradually all the others joined in, the way we did on Kirtons' bus. They sang a lot of songs I didn't know, but the last one they sang I joined in. It was *Rule Britannia*. That's what we were singing as we pulled into Euston.

The only other time I have seen so many people at a station was when we left for Northampton during the Blitz. This time nobody looked scared or lost, except, perhaps, for me. I was beginning to feel ill again and, with the huge crowds, didn't see Daddy right away; not until I heard him calling, "Margaret, Margaret. Over here," and at last we were hugging each other. We held hands as we struggled through the crowds and out to the bus stop, where, sooner than we expected, we managed to get on a bus and up to the top, to see better. It was marvelous. All of London was full of swirling crowds of happy people, many wearing fancy hats and carrying balloons. Daddy said, "They'll be going to Trafalgar Square or Buckingham Palace." I might have thought I'd like to do that, but all I wanted to do was go home. At London Bridge the only crowds were going into London, on trains as packed as mine to Euston had been. Our train out of London wasn't crowded at all. We were quickly at Hither Green, out of the station and on the last lap to 31 Handen

125

Road, with none of the qualms Mummy had when she returned alone from a weekend in Gayton.

Since I was feeling really groggy by now and went straight to my bedroom to have a nap, I don't remember much else until the evening. Mummy had told me that there was to be a party with most of their friends at Pop and Mrs. Smith's house. Pop Smith is the church organist and choirmaster. I wanted very much to be able to go, and certainly didn't want Mummy or Daddy to think they'd have to stay home with me. I slept for the whole of the rest of the day and woke up feeling elated to be there, to be going to a party and to be going with Mummy and Daddy.

It was wonderful. All the Smiths' neighbours seemed to be having parties too. The road was closed to traffic; not that there'd have been much. Hardly anybody with a car had petrol. Outside the Pop Smiths' house, there were two long trestle tables already laden with food from people who had arrived earlier, and we had brought more. After six years all the street lights were on, and were strung all the way up the road, from one side to the other, with coloured lights. I had never seen so many lights on all at once. I had never seen so much food all at once. Everyone had been saving from their rations for months. You know how sometimes, in a book written before the war, you read about a table groaning with food. These tables were. And there was singing. Most of the people were members of the church choir and some of a choral society. They knew lots and lots of songs. It was all as festive as it could possibly be, even though some of the people there have sons still away, including the Smiths, who have one who is a prisoner of war in Japan. Although they must still be very worried, they were obviously enjoying this celebration.

The absolutely best part, what made it so gloriously

festive, was the lights every where: blazing from the houses, blazing from the streetlamps, blazing from those strung between the poles. The only thing that could possibly have made it better for Mummy and Daddy and me would have been to have the boys there, but they had rung in the morning to say that they would have celebrations too, Harold at Cambridge and Gordon and Richard in Frome. I'm wondering what Richard will do with his bottle tops now. Keep setting them out until the war with Japan is won?

Addenda

1. We were all home as soon as the summer holidays began and attended a much smaller celebration of V-J Day. Before long Auntie Cissie and Auntie Jessie had found a house they liked in Cornwall, a long way away but somewhere we enjoyed for summer holidays, often taking Mary Chester with us.

2. We saw the Turners, Auntie Grace and Uncle Bill occasionally, and kept very close ties with Gayton. Auntie Olive, Uncle Aubrey, and Mary came sometimes for a weekend, and we, especially I, went to Home Farm sometimes. (As I drew near, I felt the way Mole did in *The Wind in the Willows* as he and Rat were walking back from the Wild Wood. Suddenly he felt a tug and knew he was near his home.) I loved these visits, especially waking early in the morning to the familiar farm sounds: a cock crowing, horses' hooves clattering, and rooks chattering away in the big tree behind the barn.

3. The Roes and Semples remained my good friends: Elizabeth, and sometimes Helen and Mary, visiting us and I them. Helen and Mary and I still write to each other.

4. Because my mother and father realized how little I had enjoyed Eltham Hill, where I had a scholarship, they decided to pay for me to go to Blackheath High School, where I didn't. I am truly grateful for this. I spent five

happy years there and, I think, received a better education.

5. Extensive repairs had to be done on our house. It had received no direct damage, but the high explosives, which destroyed the church next door, caused big cracks in most of our walls. Because the house was still standing and not a real danger, the repairs didn't begin for almost three years. Then there were many disruptions, upheavals, and constant noise. Each day it was like living in a very busy train station. The rest of us escaped to the office, university, or school. My mother had to endure every day.

6. Mother seemed to survive all this, added to the wartime experiences, very well, but several years later she had a nervous breakdown and would sing songs to herself about the war. By now I was married with a husband and three young children and living in the U.S. My father and brothers with their wives saw her through this difficult time, and when I next returned to England, she seemed to me to be her usual self, but she was never, after that, physically healthy. I think many "survivors" of the war must have had similar experiences.